MW01489536

This book is dedicated to Gail Solish,
who guided me through thick and thin
with wisdom, humour and compassion,
and to all survivors,
with respect and honour.

CONTENTS

FOUR: Beginning

ACKNOWLEDGEMENTS

My first thanks go to the Canada Council Explorations Program for the grant that backed me in making my vision of this book a reality. I would also like to thank Anna Miransky, Gail Solish and Jacqueline Spring for their support in the application process.

Maureen FitzGerald read a sample of the manuscript at the time I applied for the grant. Her encouragement to me, an unknown writer just beginning to believe in herself, is something I will never forget. I want to express my gratitude for this and for her continuing enthusiasm about the book.

I want to thank everyone at Women's Press. They have been friendly, helpful and accessible, making my first experience in the publishing world so positive. I especially want to thank Angela Robertson and Ann Decter. Angela deftly managed the nuts and bolts of this project from the title to your shelf. Ann, who edited the manuscript, has done a tremendous job of tightening and fine-tuning it while retaining the work's integrity and intent. This book is a deeply intimate work, and Ann and Angela have at all times shown the greatest respect and understanding. Thank you.

Finally, I want to thank Ann Brown, a dear friend who patiently listened to me read the manuscript as it progressed, providing honest and invaluable feedback. Her "ta-da" at the end of each chapter was a touchstone telling me that my faith in the recovery process had come through.

PROLOGUE:

Looking Forward, Looking Back

I look in the mirror and see a rosy, smiling face, the woman I have become from the frightened shell of five years ago. Sitting cross-legged on the floor, packing up my dictionaries for the move to my new apartment, I picture my book printed, on a shelf, in a reader's hands, your hands. I want you to know me — the little, sturdy woman with an apple face. A Jewish woman. A survivor.

As a woman, I have inherited a history of oppression; as a Jew, one of persecution. But it is also an inheritance of transcending the odds, of creativity and growth. I am proud of this history, proud of my Jewish heritage, and proud to be a part of the mystery and power of women. I am amazed at our endurance and the fruitfulness of our lives, despite being squashed, and I believe when we are not squashed, we will recreate the world.

It was hard for me to place, alongside this pride, my experience of abuse. Yet that is the truth of my life: I was abused in my Jewish family by my grandmother, my brother, and later, by my husband — sexually, physically and emotionally.

This truth was obscured not only by the secrecy inside my family, but also by misinformation outside it. When I heard that Jewish families are never abusive, I felt that there must be something terrible in me that provoked the abuse in my family. When I read that sibling incest is harmless or that female perpetrators are virtually unknown, I felt unentitled to my pain and anger, a victim of no account, ashamed and alone.

The fact is that I was not alone. While researchers have estimated that only ten percent of sexual abusers in the United States are women, their victims number 3.7 million people.[1] Research has focused on male offenders, dismissing women who abuse as rare, unusual, and unworthy of study. Does this sound familiar? Women, especially women who do not fit the social norm, are so often invisible. Instead, we are presented with myths that bind us. While it is difficult to accept women offenders, I believe that only by knowing the full range of our human nature can we dispel the myths and live freely chosen lives. Now that researchers have begun to study female perpetrators, we will get the information that we need to understand them and so to understand our own destructive and creative potential.

Similarly, sibling abuse has often been overlooked in research, and, based on anecdotal evidence, trivialized, although it appears the most common form of incest.[2] The fact is that sibling incest is not harmless. Victims of sibling incest are more likely to remain single than other incest survivors, and are more fearful of sexual assault. Fifty percent of sibling incest victims have reported violent marriages compared to eighteen percent of non-incested women.[3]

Nor are Jewish families exempt from violence. The fact is that abuse occurs in fifteen to nineteen percent of Jewish homes, religious and non-religious alike, a rate of abuse about the same as that of the general society. However, on average, non-Jewish women come forward in their twenties, after three to five years of living with violence, while Jewish women stay eight to ten years and seek help in their thirties and forties.[4] For a community that places a high value on family life, this is hard to stomach, but I believe that our values require us to confront the problem and give us the means to do it.

---

1 Anne L. Horton et al, *The Incest Perpetrator* (Newbury Park, CA: Sage Publications Inc., 1990), 119-120.
2 Ibid, 106.
3 Diana E.H. Russell, *The Secret Trauma, Incest in the Lives of Girls and Women* (New York: Basic Books, Inc., 1986), 286-287.
4 Elana Elizak Kuperstein, "Domestic Violence in the Jewish Home," *Chicago Jewish Sentinel* (November 10, 1988).

Family violence and sexual abuse cross all boundaries. To reduce the incidence and heal the damage, the facts need to be faced and the experiences of victims honoured.

No matter who abused you or the nature of the abuse, you and your experience count. Healing is possible. You are not alone. Other people have been through it and will understand. They will support and encourage you, listen to you, respect you, value you for who you really are. You do not have to be silent. You are entitled to your feelings and to live the life of your choosing. You can speak, love, cry, grow, make your corner of the world a good place.

I wrote *Ordinary Wonders* to give back something of the many gifts that were given me along the road to recovery. I had a resource I wanted to share, the words that chart my journey, words of pain and joy and discovery. I offer you my experience and understanding in the hope that it will make your journey a little easier.

It has been a year and a half since I finished *Ordinary Wonders*. I continue to heal and grow. I imagine myself many years from now, an old woman still healing and growing, discovering new things. May we all get to be old and wise and contented, relishing every bite of life.

BEFORE BEGINNING:

A Living Hell

I wouldn't have said that my life was hell. I wouldn't have said much, because I thought little and felt less. I was too busy getting through nights of abuse and tired days of work, too busy faking it. Hell was familiar. I thought it was unavoidable.

I didn't know what caring intimacy meant, and that it could exist for me. The intimacy I'd known was soul-destroying. I thought I must deserve it, and must be a "bad person." I was scared to let people know the real me, fearing that my "badness" would harm, horrify and repel them. Eugene, my husband, played on my fears and ignorance so that I felt worse about myself. He punished me whenever I spent time with friends. He violently insisted that people I liked were out to get him or me, or were guilty of some sin he concocted. If I were foolish enough to invite them over, his belligerence and crudeness often drove them away. I blamed myself, becoming further removed from the people who could have told me I was living in hell. I thought Eugene was the only one who could bear to live with such a horrible person as I was, and that if he left me, I would be alone forever.

My parents tried to tell me, but I was angry with them. They had done their best. They had loved me. But their love and their best had not protected me, had not seen me as I was, had not given me what I needed. Lonely, grieving, I dreamt that marriage would save me. When Eugene wanted me, and my parents criticized him, my resentment toward them exploded. I thought I was hostile because my parents hated him. They thought I was hostile because Eugene hated them. So we all avoided the truth about my childhood.

My life did not look like hell to my colleagues and casual acquaintances. They saw a competent, cheerful professional. They couldn't know that the largest part of me was occupied with apologizing, trying to be better and failing, being terrified of abandonment, supporting Eugene and making ends meet by a miracle, begging him not to leave me, as he did weekly.

Every once in a long while it occurred to me that I couldn't always be wrong. I couldn't be that "bad." But when I was upset Eugene told me that I looked happy. When I disliked something he said that I liked it. When I felt good, he said that I'd messed up. He was so sure, so loudly and threateningly sure, that I was convinced I didn't know my own mind. I must be crazy. If I wasn't yet, his torment would make me crazy. I couldn't stand it. Then I'd haul up my socks, tell myself I could stand it, and did. To bear it, I let go of what was most alive in me: writing, friendship, music, beauty, fun, laughter, love, social conscience, hope, vision. Eugene demanded it. I gave.

Despite my depression and loneliness, despite exhaustion and abuse — so familiar and so crushing — there was a small part of me that was indomitable, a part of me that could see beyond abuse to something good.

This part brought me back from the brink of being completely absorbed by Eugene, just as it saved me from being absorbed by the abuse in my childhood. It directed me to build my strength and independence step by tiny step. I went to night school. I studied. I made friends at work. I became a chartered accountant — Eugene's idea, like all of his ideas, riding roughshod over my inclinations. Counting instead of writing, bosses instead of independence, suits instead of jeans. But training as a C.A. student put me in an environment in which I was consistently treated with respect for the first time in my life. I was valued. I was working toward a goal. I could see that I was good at what I was doing and that built self-respect. It gave me a concrete focus in the midst of chaos, widening my horizons at a time when my life had narrowed to surviving tonight's fight.

I suffered so much domination in my personal life that I had a low tolerance for being told what to do at work. Although I couldn't admit how completely my family and Eugene controlled me, I felt my desire to work on my own as an urgent need. Throughout the years of overtime and study, I was propelled by the dream of opening my own office. When finally I did, I adored being my own boss, and made money too. But not enough money to support Eugene in the style to which he insisted. I increased credit to save my practice, even though I knew it was doomed unless Eugene contributed something. I wanted so badly to keep my practice going that I overcame my fears of being cursed and deserted. I asked Eugene to get a job. He refused. Six months later I went back to being an employee, up to my eyeballs in debt, carrying the lease on an empty office.

I was angry. I'd lost my dream, and it was clear even to my muddled, squashed mind that it would have succeeded had Eugene not been a dead weight.

I was unable to recognize that I'd been abused. I was unaware that the abuse in my marriage mirrored my childhood. I was still apologetic, still confused, but I was angry and I knew it. I was angry enough to begin telling my good friend Ann about my life as it really was. Talking to her broke the trap of isolation. She validated my feelings. She supported me. She warmed me.

I still imagined that I was at fault for my relationship with Eugene, for my anger, for my pain. I still thought I must be crazy. But as I saw my thirtieth birthday just up ahead, I couldn't accept that this misery was it for the duration. I suggested marriage counselling to Eugene, as I had previously on occasion. This time though, I was prepared to go on my own if necessary. My firmness was an indicator that I was breaking free and for the first time Eugene agreed to counselling. His meal ticket was threatened, his arms and his legs. He lived through me as if I were his puppet, and now his puppet was walking away. By small steps I had grown strong enough to chance Eugene's rage. I could risk his leaving me because I wanted more from life than what I had and believed that I was entitled to it.

I still wanted to make my marriage work, mistaking abuse for love. I couldn't yet look myself or my life in the face. But when my marriage counsellor recommended individual therapy, I saw it as a lifeline and I grabbed it. I was ready to begin.

ONE

Beginning

Ī

Fury on Ice

To survive abuse inflicted by our families, we forget it and minimize it. We numb ourselves to the pain of it. Recovery from emotional, physical or sexual abuse is a process of remembering and feeling. We reclaim the good things about ourselves and our lives as we experience and face the damaging, painful things.

I survived by forgetting that my grandmother abused me physically and sexually. I called my brother's sexual abuse child play and overlooked the extensive abuse in my marriage. I blamed myself for whatever I couldn't forget or ignore. I was the keeper of the family problems, the outcast, the crazy who lived in another city while my brother, my sister and my parents lived within a three-mile radius of each other.

They called me the quiet one, and I was — stunned by abuse, forced to be quiet by the bad things that happened when I wasn't. I wrapped myself in a cocoon of silence, numbing the anger, pain and loss that I was too young to handle. In my cocoon, I felt safe from the hostile world that my outer self negotiated, but I was also removed from the life I wanted so desperately.

Once in therapy, I began to feel. Though I didn't feel much at first, it was overwhelming compared to numbness, discomforting, frightening and unfamiliar. I didn't know what to do with my feelings, where to put them. I didn't know how to talk and feel at the same time. My personal history had taught me that if I spoke out, terrible things would happen. My feelings might destroy me or the world or Gail, my therapist.

When Gail proposed writing as an outlet, I felt as if she gave me back my good arm, lost when I stopped writing during my marriage.

I realized how much writing, and the loss of it, had meant to me. Years of silence poured out as fast as I could write. Though I was still too scared to speak from my inner self, I was able to communicate what I remembered, believed, dreamt and feared by giving Gail copies of my journal and reading aloud from it.

I began this journal a month or so after I started therapy, my first night in an incest survivors' group. Engulfed by vivid impressions, I recalled Gail's suggestion, made that afternoon, to write out my thoughts and feelings. Sitting at a rickety wooden table in the basement of the YWCA, outside the daycare room in which we'd met, I scribbled furiously on a scrap of paper. The next day I bought a notebook and glued this scrap to the first page of my journal.

Initially I had no interest in joining the group, but my feelings changed when my brother came to town and invited me out for dinner. Gail had to cancel my appointment the same week, something she rarely did. I felt lost and panicky. I wanted to avoid my brother, but was scared to say no. I asked my friend Ann for advice. She didn't understand what it meant to come from a family like mine, and I wasn't yet capable of telling her, so her sensible suggestions didn't ease my panic. I decided to tell my sister Ellen about the incest. I made up my mind to join the group. And I told Ted, my brother, that I wasn't available for dinner.

Ellen's belief and compassion, though it was on again, off again, felt good while it lasted. It reinforced my decision to look for more support in the survivors' group. I had no idea how difficult group would be, though Gail warned me. I poo-pooed her warnings. I was tough. I'd heard worse, I said, from my parents, who were Holocaust survivors. I didn't realize that hearing abused women talk about their feelings would be so powerful because we were alike, that the horrors they survived were also mine. Nothing in my life could measure up to the epic tragedy of the Holocaust. My parents' lives were still more meaningful to me than my own. Because of what they had survived, I saw them as the unjudgeable saints who transcended horror. Keeping my eyes on their past enabled me to deny the horror of my own.

Group therapy confronted me with the reality of incest, unavoidably painful and frightening. But group also provided a place outside both my family and my marriage, a place in which I could begin to see myself through other people's eyes. Group opened possibilities that hadn't previously existed, possibilities for self-expression, relationships, acceptance and feeling. I really began therapy when I started group, April 22, 1986. I was scared to death and believed I didn't belong because what had happened to me wasn't that bad. Yet I was also enabled to break my silence in the way most natural to me, by beginning my journal.

1986

APRIL 22

We are nine. Nine women sit in a circle of hurt, of fury on ice. I would like to hold each of you, to rock you and comfort you, to erase the years of anguish, sweat and pain. I could be strong and articulate for you, but for myself I am frozen. I am numb, my eyes full of tears. Are these tears mine? What do they say? I have no words. I borrow yours. Like a drumbeat I hear:

If I am not for myself, who will be for me?
But if I am only for myself, what am I?
And if not now, when?[1]

I feel your anger, betrayal, fear, denial, helplessness. I borrow your words. I borrow your feelings — "Yes, that's me!" I am excited. I live; the shadow that is a controller, lecturer, businesswoman fills out. Blank greyness turns to blue eyes, brown hair. When the meeting ends, I stand in the empty corridor, exhilaration fading in the silence; words, feelings abandoned. A grey shadow flits through the night.

---

1   A proverb of Hillel, the greatest sage of the Second Temple period, a humble man of peace.

APRIL 24

This need to read, write, talk sometimes feels as if it will consume me. Today I am bone-tired and nothing seems real. I hope if I read and write enough, the malignant spots on my soul will be excised.

Sometimes I think I'm being self-indulgent. All this looking inward and focusing on feelings, reasons, the past, seems nauseatingly self-centred. Why can't I forget and move on?

APRIL 28

I feel so terribly sick — my stomach's in agony. I don't think getting things out in the open is worth it if I'm going to be in this much pain.

The anxiety was gone by about 9:00, giving way to depression. Pain or numbness, what a choice. I can't face what happened and I can't face the terrible aloneness. I want my Mummy to make it all better, to hold and protect me. But she won't and she never did.

I need help to cope. I thought I was stronger than I am. I'm tired of mixing up Eugene and Ted in my dreams, my memories.

MAY 1

I am violently angry at myself for calling Gail.

"You slut, you god-damned whore! What makes you think *you* have the right to get help from someone? You stinking shitbag, you don't deserve it. Stand on your own two feet."

I'm scared I'm going to explode. I'm scared that I am like the girl in the movies who looks beautiful from behind, but turns out to be a grinning, decomposing corpse. There must be a monster inside me, otherwise why would my brother pick on me? If I don't hold myself tight that monster will break out. The me that I know will crumple to the ground, a fragile paper mask torn apart.

MAY 3

I think about Gail kneeling beside me, saying so intently that it was Ted's fault, that my soul is not warped. This image makes me feel very shaky.

MAY 6

I expected that I would see a therapist, read a couple of books, talk a little, and presto — a cure. Lilian is all better. Instead I feel sick, and wonder if the "cure" is worse than the "disease."

I love Eugene so much. I'm lucky to have found him, or we're lucky we found each other. I am ashamed of myself for being so wrapped up in my own misery.

MAY 20

I'm shivering after seeing Gail. I want to not be. Or to explode. Or to be numb. I don't like the tension, the feeling of things trying to get out, pushing at the walls of my skin from inside. For God's sake, come out and let me be.

I just have to wait and let my feelings out little by little. You can do it. Breathe slowly. It's okay.

I want to think about what was said to me in group tonight: there's something in me people respond to; I'm understanding, tactful, eloquent, to the point. My parents always said I was intolerant, undiplomatic, unobservant, unable to take criticism and poor at interacting with people.

MAY 21

I wish someone would tell me that I could go to bed and cover my head with blankets and not come out until I was good and ready.

MAY 23

The complications that arise if I'm not a bad person:
> My parents failed me.
> I love them.
> They love me.
> They don't know me.
> They know some of me very well.
> I hate them.
> I am angry at them.
> I am alone. A solitary rock.
> I am not alone. I am worthy of being cared for.

If I reach out, I may not be rejected.

I can be sexual.

My feelings will not horrify or overwhelm everybody.

Ted is a worm. He disgusts me. I hate him.

I am sorry for him.

I love Ellen. I'm angry that she doesn't support me.

MAY 26

Therapy is a road. As I walk along, I'm getting muscle cramps because I'm not used to walking. I'm barefoot. My feet are soft and I walk on rocks. I don't know where I'm going. I'm scared of what I see. I'm open to the feel of earth and stone, wind blowing, smell of sewers and pine trees, sound of thunder and birdsong. So much it makes my head hurt. I look around in wonder. I stumble in fear. I can reach out to steady myself, or lean on someone. I can pause. But I can't close myself against the smells, the sounds, the feel of it. I'm too old now. There's no mother to pick me up as an infant and carry me along peeking through her arms. The stones are sharp. I hobble and can't wait till my feet toughen. To stand and lean against Gail would hardly touch the pain. I'd rather keep going. But I do want to talk about what I see. I need to be heard.

MAY 28

Is this really worth it? What will my life be like? Pain to the end of time? And against that, the moments of excitement, of feeling that I'm alive and anything can happen: the world is new and young.

II

A *Golem*

Those early days in therapy were awful. I pounded myself into the ground to meet the demands of work, debts, and my marriage. Reawakened memories and feelings piled on misery, and I didn't yet have new strengths and pleasures to compensate. How little good there seems to be as I re-read my journal. I thought heaven would be twenty-four hours free of anxiety. Still, I celebrated the little good I found. I had hope. I kept going. Why? How?

I understood that the terrible memories and feelings therapy brought to the surface had been inside me for years, poisoning my life. I believed that I couldn't get rid of that poisonous stuff unless I faced it. I already had survived the real thing — abuse, secrecy, betrayal, powerful feelings I'd had to bury. And I'd survived on my own. Now I had help from Gail and support from the women in group. Gail told me I wasn't alone. She said there was a way out of horror. I knew nothing about trust or being cared for or feeling liked and appreciated, but I believed Gail. I intended to use everything in me to find the way out of horror.

There have been more times than I can count when I thought I couldn't or wouldn't or didn't want to go on. Times when I felt bitter because I had not only had to suffer the original abuse but the replay too, while the abusers seemed to suffer nothing. But always the indomitable part of me led me from despair to look at the little good growing. And I was writing again. If nothing else, I had my good arm back. That was a blessing beyond measure.

My dreams were also a blessing, though they seemed to be a curse. Every night I was awakened by nightmares that scared me and wore me out. While I could numb myself and forget during the day, my night life screamed out everything I denied. I paid attention to my dreams. I talked about them. I was proud of them as something unusual and special about me, even while I felt plagued by them. Despite all my interest, I didn't understand my dreams.

When I started therapy, I could hardly keep up with the thoughts and feelings in my conscious mind, never mind attend to my dreams. Yet believing that something important spoke to me through my sleeping self, I wrote down my dreams for the day when I was able to understand their meaning.

*　*　*　*　*

MAY 29

A dream last night: There was a child molester case. The cops were asking me about Eugene. He didn't know he was suspected. Gail asked me questions too, then went to speak to my family doctor. She came back and told me there was nothing to worry about, though the doctor had done some tests I wasn't ready to know about. I was left feeling scared and ignorant.

MAY 31

I took three days off work as a break from responsibility, to hide from the world, but I let the world intrude. I can't bear my pain, but I tried to absorb Eugene's pain and my friends' pain. I berate myself because I think I haven't done it well enough. At the same time I have the joy of support from the women in group, I have the burden of their confidences. I feel I don't give enough. And I scream inside myself, "I can't bear it any more. Please God help me!"

I imagine sitting in Gail's office, hands over my head, curled in a silent ball, not drawing a breath.

I've got to figure out a way to reduce the level of stress.

JUNE 2

I had a dream about my brother I don't remember. Then I dreamt I was raped and mutilated by a concert pianist, who was my lover.

I am very, very cold. I managed well this morning. Efficient. A little voice says "Don't give up. Don't be numb." I'm not capable of being truly numb any more. I can feel a tight fist of tears in my chest. I feel embarrassed, ashamed, worthless: my parents think I'm nuts, maybe they're right. I feel like a sun imploding. Will I become a black hole, the ultimate nothingness?

JUNE 6

I'm angry that Gail was right about my inability to immunize myself against the feelings that arise in group. I'm angry that she recognized my weakness, or maybe my humanness.

I'm used to packaging my feelings and experiences in neat, labelled boxes. Sometimes the feelings become a *Golem* [1]; they burst from their confinement and shake me. "Let us out. We won't sit in that cramped little box." I shake until I can contain them again.

My boss said he was bothered by the fact that I keep my office door closed. It makes him feel I am unapproachable. He says I have to leave it open. Having my door closed has been the way I've coped with my anxiety at work. I feel so vulnerable. My stomach hurts and I'm almost in tears. I'm scared. I feel threatened, invaded.

I left work early, came home, talked to Eugene, asked him to hold me. He held me while I slept. It felt really good. When I woke up, he said, "You're awake? Good. Let's neck." I said, "I don't want to pay to be held." I've always paid before. Now I'm paying for saying no. He is distant and cold. Home is no refuge. I have no comfort. Unless I pay promptly.

We're fighting again. Eugene said I'm always feeling this and feeling that. He said I shouldn't offer sex in a way that's unenjoyable. I told him I should have just continued to say no. He didn't like that. I'm tired of being compared to his mother, who abused him. I'm no good at work. I'm no good at home. Maybe my family is right, I'm

---

1 In Jewish folklore, a *Golem* is lump of clay that is brought to life by the use of holy names. It was made to be a servant, but, growing, it breaks out of that role, taking on a life of its own.

just crazy and plain no good. Therapy is like trying to make a silk purse out of a sow's ear.

JUNE 11

I'm so excited I'm going to burst. Eugene found some old writings of mine: a diary, poems, and some stories I wrote between sixteen and twenty. I'm good! I was stunned. The last couple of stories were really good!

I've found a part of me I thought lost.

JUNE 13

The problem with sex is that when I do Eugene off, a nightly event, I don't want to be touched in any form. As I get tired and wrack my brain for a way to make him come, I get hostile and want to punch his face in. I know it's bad for us, the suppressed anger, repulsion, compliance, all kinds of tensions. On the other hand, changes are scary for Eugene. If I suddenly put my foot down now, I think he'd feel threatened. We would fight a lot. Maybe this should go on the back burner for a while.

JUNE 15

Sideroad 9 and Concession 19, over a fence and in a wild field. I relieved some anger by throwing two loads of stones. I imagined my parents and my brother drowning, pleading piteously for help. I was merciless.

If you could see this place: the pond reflecting trees and bush, purple and white flowers, the hills, great leafy trees and mosquitos and grasshoppers and birds, reeds five feet high. This place can take my anger and absorb it unharmed, life unbroken. On the way here we stopped on an old bridge over a creek. We saw little yellow birds with black wings, in the distance green on green — hills, field, lush woods.

JUNE 16

I think I'm hideously ugly.

JUNE 17

When I think about anger, I see a head slowly turning, a howl of rage and pain. I turn away. I say no to the vision.

Gail asked me when I was going to fall apart.

...What a wonderful world! The branches of a maple and an elm overhang my seat on this rock. The twigs are so delicate, the leaves absolutely marvelous.

JUNE 20

Gail said that Eugene and I are boring in our intensity and that I've lost my sense of humour about myself. I can't believe that I am boring and humourless sometimes about some things. Oh no. I must be perfect. If I'm not perfect, I am bad. I am a boring, humourless person, and that's all I am. Everything positive that Gail or anyone else has said about me is a lie, because how can those good qualities survive in this grey soul. Am I ever blown up with my own importance. I am unique. I am the only one of four billion people who can't be a mixed bag of good and bad. If I can't be perfect, I may as well lie down and die because nothing less is acceptable.

JUNE 24

I feel like I'm pushing with all my might against a brick wall. I'm angry and frustrated. I beat my hands against the wall until they're scraped and sore. Then I hang my head and cry. Superwoman fails again.

Take it easy. Be patient. Pretend you're someone else. Be gentle. Remember where you were two months ago. You've been able to feel. You've rediscovered writing. You've heard a lot of nice things about yourself and been able to accept them, occasionally. You've recognized some limitations. You've expressed anger. You've made new friends. You're learning to find moments of joy, to create these moments in the woods, listening to music. There's a whole world opening up for you. You can't discover it all just like that. It'll come. Take your time.

JUNE 26

7:15 a.m. A dream: in Gail's office there was a desk, a couch and a clock where time was marked in red. We were sitting on the couch. I dilly-dallied for twenty minutes. Then I said I wanted to discuss my parents, but instead I started to talk about my grandmother. I said she wrote (though she didn't in reality) and travelled. Then I started screaming. I screamed and screamed. In the middle I said, "Gail, I'm really scared." Gail was holding my hand and had an arm around me. I screamed for half an hour. Then Gail said it was time to stop. I was really shook up. She was very distant and went to her desk. She told me that the only time she had for an appointment was 10:30 at night. I said fine. She looked surprised and I woke up.

JUNE 27

I am scared a lot of the time now, but it's not nearly as bad as it used to be. I'm more accustomed to feeling. I'm scared about:

1. New patterns of thought; trying to find the middle road between jumping off a cliff and hiding in bed; not having to be perfect; trying to hear good things.

2. My dream of screaming about my grandmother. It may presage nothing. But I feel as if I'm on the edge of something.

3. Soliciting business for my practice.

JUNE 28

Sitting at 10th and 19th Sideroads above a brook. Across the road three horses and a colt are following a cow around the field. The colt looks so funny when it runs: spindly legs a bit wobbly on the take-off. Up the hill a flock of white sheep and one lone black one are nibbling grass and butting each other.

JUNE 30

As I was falling asleep, I pictured myself in Gail's office. She asked me where I was. I said, "I am five. I am five." Then I started screaming "Mama!"

The summer I turned five my mother and brother were in Israel and I was alone with my grandmother. We always called my grandmother, "Mama." She lived with us until she remarried when I was twelve, though she was gone quite a bit from the time I was ten — off looking for a husband.

III

The Soft White Spider

JULY 15

WHERE DID YOU GO?

Soft wind soughing in the trees,
Curled around purple flowers, orange striped bees,
And in the whisper of the wind and in the scent of flowers
Sways a silken web, dainty strands of power.

Silver threads glinting in the sun,
Web of trust, web of tears, out of pain was spun
And in the centre of the web and in the twisted core
Squats the well-fed spider always craving more.

Small fly twisting on a thread —
Where are you now? Left for dead
While the soft white spider spins a new
And better web, sweet flies to catch with sweeter glue.

You small fly, wings ripped away,
Who does she remind you of, where are you today?
All alone within the web, trapped by threads of silk,
Dream of days that never were, dream of mother's milk.

*   *   *   *   *

I meant to write this poem as a mean kind of joke, mocking Gail by
incorporating the phrases that she typically used during my sessions.
What I ended up writing was totally different from my design. I

30

discovered that, no matter what my intentions, writing revealed my true thoughts and feelings. The poem was no joke.

"Where Did You Go?" exposed the truth of my position in the family — abused, abandoned, outraged, powerless, hurt, trapped by false hopes. When I wrote it, however, I saw it simply as an expression of my anger toward Gail for going on holiday and continued to see it that way for a long time. Yet I didn't write another poem during my first year in therapy. Poetry revealed too much. I wasn't ready for such intimacy with myself.

Recovery is a huge task: healing the hurts, learning and unlearning, saying all the unsaid things, getting to know who you are and what you want. I think that each of us has an internal regulator which determines the pace at which our awareness grows. It is a pace that allows us to cope effectively with our discoveries. Sometimes we stop ourselves. Sometimes we push too hard. Respecting our pace is one of the ways in which we can repair the damage we experienced as children, when we weren't allowed to develop naturally but were stopped and pushed according to the whim of irresponsible adults.

The idea that I could pace myself was still beyond me. I was running headlong into disaster, overworked and overtired, juggling a full-time job, freelance work, group, marriage counselling, and therapy twice a week. I couldn't listen to the signals in my dreams or my body aches, even in my journal, because I was still in an abusive situation. To tolerate that abuse, and to keep from being overwhelmed by the way in which it repeated my childhood, I had to stay out of touch with most of myself.

I was caught in a push-pull that was tearing me up. I wanted the truth, but was unable, yet, to deal with it. I pushed myself to read everything contained in the literature on abuse and to do at once everything it said about recovery. At the same time I was unable to apply most of what I read to my present life. I was caught between wanting to be a good girl for Gail and for Eugene. Somewhere in the middle of all that compliance was real growth and desire to be myself. The conflict between my awareness and old patterns of compliance is reflected in the way I wrote about Eugene. One page shows intense hatred, the next is nauseatingly solicitous. This incongruity, however, was a step up from total silence and pretence. As my awareness grew, the push-pull lessened and I was able to write more often about the reality of my marriage. From writing about it to acting on it was not a great distance.

*   *   *   *   *

JULY 19

I know I'm not responsible for Eugene's moods, but I feel that if only I could figure out the right thing to do, I could put him in a better mood. I tried cuddling — that worked for one minute. Then I suggested making love. That didn't work. I asked him what I could do to make him feel better: no answer. I apologized about five times. He's reading the newspaper, sighing. It makes me want to tear my hair out and scream.

I feel trapped. Everything is my responsibility. It's my duty to make Eugene sleep. How do I change that? I just cry and cry. If I leave the apartment, for sure the son of a bitch will stay awake. Tomorrow will be destroyed.

I don't want to do anything, any more. It makes no difference if I try to lessen the pressure I'm under, because I'm just not good enough, not good for anything. How do I get out of this?

Eugene is oh so reasonable. All he wants is to relax, poor boy. My bitching and crying won't let him. I cried quietly, but he heard me close the door. I hate myself. I feel like garbage. I want to go home, but I have no home.

JULY 20

6:00 a.m. I tried. I really did. I went to sleep. Eugene came back every ten minutes to wake me up. I talked and went back to sleep. He woke me up again. I said we're both at fault, and my staying awake wouldn't help either of us. I went back to sleep. He woke me up, and I said it again. And again. Until finally I lost my temper and yelled and slammed the bedroom door. What did I do wrong? How can I avoid this?

Eugene came back and said he wanted to separate. He asked me for how long. I told him that since he wanted to separate, he should tell me. He said he didn't know yet. Fine. I tried to get back to sleep. He didn't get a big enough rise out of me so he came back in five minutes to talk about the keys. What a cutey! There has to be a better way to handle this, but I'm at a loss.

8:30 am. I'm in the car. Eugene woke me up again. I asked him if he wanted a massage. He said, "no, go back to sleep." Next thing, he says he'll be home at 1:00 pm. I said fine. After he repeated it three times and I didn't jump, he said he'd be home sometime tonight. I finally woke up. I'm going out. Eugene is at home, playing with the computer.

Eugene was asleep when I got home. After he woke up, I asked him if he'd like to drive out to the country. We are now in stage three (or is it four or five)? The GUILT stage. Eugene is never going to the country because we always fight beforehand. We have also fought before and after doing everything else, so by that token we'd never do anything. If I ignore this one, the next stage will be "we might as well break up. There's nothing else."

In the park. This "not fighting" is leaving me as tired as fighting, except that at least I've got out of the apartment and enjoyed the day a bit.

Eugene followed me to the park to fight. He asked me what I wanted and I said I'd like to do something together. I asked him what he'd like me to do to make him feel better. He kept repeating that he wants me to give a shit, which I do. Then he walked away. Oh now he's coming back. Presumably this is for the breaking up speech.

It was. He picked at me and picked at me until I started screaming and crying and making a spectacle of myself. Then he was satisfied that I cared. His insecurity is going to kill me. I would like to tear him apart. I hate him. There's no getting away from it. I told him that everything was fine. The fight was not serious. It was just a replay of nothings. We're supposed to do something together in half an hour. Can we have a torture-and-maim-your-husband party?

JULY 23

Once in a long while when I feel sexual I'll come on to Eugene. Normally he loses interest.

Mostly I fake, but every so often, when I feel it's been too long, I get some sort of satisfaction. At times I feel sexual, I usually just ignore it. I feel a million times worse trying to make love when I need to and ending up in a brawl.

JULY 25

I'm sad. I feel helpless in my dependency on Gail. I can't wait for the time when that dependency will end and I'm scared it won't. I feel abandoned, rejected, lost like a little kid. I need Gail and I don't like that. The loss reminds me of some time I can't remember; whatever it is that causes my fear that I'll be left.

It's hard for me to know whether I'm just touchy over my writing or whether I'm responding legitimately to Eugene's attacks. Whenever he talks about it, I feel as if he's trespassing. He's walking along the fence bordering my soul and I'm afraid he'll jump over the fence and trample it into formless mud. Eugene doesn't read my journal, can't control it. I think he fears what he doesn't know about me, but, reasonably, he asks me how he can possibly take anything away from me.

AUGUST 5

I had a nightmare last night about a mass murderer who cut people up into little pieces. I was a detective, looking for him.

AUGUST 6

Ellen tells me that she feels in the middle. She is pissed off. She thinks I want her to side with me against the rest of the family. I told her I don't but she didn't believe me. I suggested we don't discuss anything relating to the family. She liked that, though she said she felt bad because she knew I needed it. I told her I have other people to talk to. I liked being open and honest because I felt closer to her. I said I loved her. I said I was angry.

AUGUST 7

I feel like I've survived Gail's holiday. Eugene has been very supportive.

AUGUST 14

Something Gail said to think about: I need to learn to give to myself and take from other people to replenish myself.

AUGUST 15

I think it's time to start dealing with the incest, so all my defenses are flying up. I'm mad at Gail. What's the point of telling her anything? I'm mad at myself. I'm a bad, stupid person. I'm irresponsible. I'm a spoilt brat and I should shape up.

I'm mad at Eugene because he forgot my birthday. God protect me from my anger. I'm afraid.

The snake curls around the tree, red eyes, tongue flicking as it hisses sweetly. "Come to me, my pretty. Come and be a woman." The child's curiosity has it lean against the tree and look up at the snake. "Say yes, my dear. What do you say?" The child looks at its feet, finger on its mouth. The snake undulates along the tree. Scales rasp bark. The snake curls around the child. "Would you like to see, to know, to be a good girl?" The child curls a finger in its hair and shrugs. "You don't say no, do you?" The child pauses. The snake croons as it wraps around the child, tickling it gently. Then the snake wraps tighter, squeezes, chokes until it feels a pliable lifeless body in its grasp. The child falls. The snake crawls along its length, wriggling along legs, stomach, chest, and croaks, "You're a woman now."

AUGUST 17

Laying in the sun among purple flowers, a bath of sun. The sky is such a hot blue, it looks like the sky in Israel. As I lean back and look up at the sky and the dragonfly circling overhead, it seems to me a perfect day from someone's dream. On a patch of bare earth, nearby, I see what looks like a long dried-up brown bug. When I move, it flies away — a beautiful moth with velvet black wings. Four turtles are sunning themselves on a rock in the pond.

AUGUST 25

A life that has warm cats sitting on your lap, rubbing their noses in your face, lifting their heads for a kiss, such a life is worth the aching in my heart.

AUGUST 29

I don't know how long I can wait to see if Eugene changes: one year, five, ten? In the meantime I'm bitchy and feel trapped. We can't have kids like this. Oh God, I don't know what to do.

Eugene and I talked things over. He finally seemed to understand what I meant by feeling suffocated because he lives through me. He said he would try to be more separate. We'll see. Eugene promises a lot in his insecurity, the same way I have when I've been afraid that he'll leave me. I'm very tired, sad, spiritless.

AUGUST 30

Eugene and I were up most of the night. He woke me up to do him off, but couldn't get to sleep afterward. He said he was uptight. Before he fell asleep, I told him I was going to lunch with Ann. I asked if that was okay and he said yes. I hope when I get back, he doesn't fight with me, again.

SEPTEMBER 2

Eugene is trying so hard to do what I want him to in order not to suffocate me. His efforts make me want to scream because he's still so tied to me, into me. That's unfair because what more can he do than change the way he acts. I'm confused and scared and mad. Why so mad? I don't know. I feel trapped and squeezed and my mind can't breathe. I'm drowning. I don't want to drown.

SEPTEMBER 5

I used to think I was a boring person. I thought I would never enjoy anything, never live. But I do enjoy life when I'm alone or with people other than Eugene. Our fights, his attacks on my sexuality and personality ("you're inconsiderate, a cunt, a castrating bitch"), the burden of responsibility, burnt the life out of me and left an anger so violent I became numb.

SEPTEMBER 7

Ruth and I went out for brunch, then played Monopoly at her place. I wasn't eager to go home. Eugene greeted me with monosyllables and red eyes.

SEPTEMBER 8

I suggested last night that Eugene and I separate for a week. He asked me to take it back and I did.

IV

Bontsha the Silent

I believe it's no coincidence that I began to think about the story "Bontsha The Silent" just after my aborted attempt at separation. Like Bontsha, I was so crushed that ordinary things seemed to be fantastic favours. I believed that Eugene was supportive during Gail's holiday because for two weeks he didn't keep me up at night, fighting. I was unfamiliar with common decency and consideration. I thought being abused was normal, a lack of abuse was kindness. The story described my silence and oppression:

At last from the judge's chair a new voice rises, loving, tender. "Bontsha my child, Bontsha" — the voice swells like a great harp — "my heart's child ..."

Within Bontsha his very soul begins to weep. He would like to open his eyes, to raise them, but they are darkened with tears. It is so sweet to cry. Never until now has it been sweet to cry.

... "My child," the judge begins again, "you have always suffered, and you have always kept silent. There isn't one secret place in your body without its bleeding wound; there isn't one secret place in your soul without its wound and blood. And you never protested. You always were silent. There in that other world, no one understood you. You never understood yourself. You never understood that you need not have been silent, that you could have cried out and that your outcries would have brought down the world itself and ended it. You never understood your sleeping strength. There in that other world, that world of lies, your silence was never rewarded, but here in paradise is the world of truth... Everything is yours!... Choose! Take! Whatever you want! You will only take what is yours!"

38

... "Well then" — and Bontsha smiles for the first time — "well then, what I would like, Your Excellency, is to have, every morning for breakfast, a hot roll with fresh butter."

A silence falls upon the great hall, and it is more terrible than Bontsha's has ever been, and slowly the judge and the angels bend their heads in shame at this unending meekness they have created on earth.

Then the silence is shattered. The prosecutor laughs aloud, a bitter laugh."[1]

Though he'd been unable to say a word against Bontsha, the prosecutor had won. Bontsha was punished by his own inability to let go of oppression, even in paradise. The end of the story haunted me through the years. I hated it, though I didn't understand and didn't know how to change it.

"Bontsha the Silent" presented me with the challenge of finding a different ending. It asked whether I too was stuck in my oppression. I had alternatives I didn't have as a child. Could I assume my rights of freedom and choice? Would I fulfil my potential? Or would I give my abusers their final victory by clinging to the familiar role of victim? The decision was mine.

*   *   *   *   *

SEPTEMBER 9

When I first read "Bontsha the Silent" as a kid, it sent shivers up my spine, but I didn't understand why. I read it over and over, the story of a man who endured agony all his life, until finally, in heaven, he was honoured for his goodness by God and the angels. And yet he remained oppressed, even when offered the treasures of heaven, unable to ask for anything more than bread and butter.

---

1   I.L. Peretz,"Bontsha the Silent,"in *Selected Stories* (New York: Schocken Books, 1974), 76-77.

What is there about me that caused the incest? It must be my fault. I can't accept it was the fault of the abuser. I can't face the anger such a thought would generate.

SEPTEMBER 13
We went to Sabbath services this morning. I felt good to bursting, and I thought — what did I do to deserve this happiness? Get born. Then I suddenly felt worn out, wondering whether I'll make it to the end.

I enjoyed sex last night. What a difference being able to say no makes. I feel warm toward Eugene today. I'm more hopeful about our future.

SEPTEMBER 14
Awful dreams last night. I dreamt over and over about Gail abandoning me, and about a great flood. Eugene and I were to meet in the small town he was from if we survived the flood. We kept getting separated. I tried to protect my baby daughter. In one of the dreams the flood was on its way. There was going to be a tremendous rush of water and I was trying to find a spot to wait where I had the best chance of survival.

SEPTEMBER 16
Gail has put me on a stress reduction program. I agreed not to write about my feelings for a while and not to read any serious books. I'm to set weekly work goals, and keep a list of the enjoyable things I do every day. I'm not going back to the next session of group.

SEPTEMBER 17
I just had a terrible nightmare. I dreamt that Gail was in the living room. I was in the bedroom with another therapist, Helene. We were sitting on Mama's (my grandmother's) bed. Helene was trying to get me to remember something. She thought maybe what I couldn't remember was a sexual experience with a girlfriend, and was trying to trigger me with her name. I got really scared and started to hyperventilate. She stopped because it had got out of hand. I kept

getting more and more scared, crying and screaming. Helene wanted to give me a pill, an anti-depressant. I said no, I didn't need it. Then I thought of writing, but I'd promised Gail I wouldn't write. So I went further and further into the fear. I was screaming, "Mama, Mama help me," but she was part of the fear. Whatever I was afraid of was focused around her, but I had no one else to turn to. Then I decided to hell with the promise, but it was too late. I couldn't write. I screamed and cried. Finally I called out, "Helene, help me back." But it was too late. She couldn't. Then I woke up, disoriented.

OCTOBER 9

On the way to meet Ruth, I saw a flock of birds very high up, swirling around as they changed directions, then breaking off in groups that flew south. I was thankful to God for showing me something so beautiful, but I still don't intend to fast on Yom Kippur. [2] I definitely don't want to ask God's forgiveness. I forgot that Monday was Yom Kippur when I arranged to meet Mary for lunch and, given a choice between a fun afternoon chatting with Mary, and fasting, chatting with Mary wins hands down. At least this time.

OCTOBER 10

I'm thinking more seriously about separation. Despite some improvements, I'm still basically unhappy in our relationship. The contrast between my moods at home and my moods away from Eugene is much sharper now that I'm putting more energy into doing what I enjoy. I'm also struck by two things that Gail said. She thinks that before we started on this stress reduction strategy, I was headed for a breakdown, possibly hospitalization. She said I've been living with a battering ram. While I'm working so hard to focus on the positive things in my life, Eugene keeps forcing doom and gloom down my throat.

I'm very volatile on this subject. I still hope that things will work out between us.

---

2   Jewish day of Atonement

OCTOBER 14

Ann was working in the neighbourhood yesterday and we met for coffee. I had a great time. She gave me some ideas on soliciting business. I was really excited when I met Eugene, told him all about it, something I haven't been doing lately. We ended up in a spat. I felt miserable. It was the nth plus one time I went from being happy to miserable around him.

I talked to Eugene about separating. He asked me not to break up for a month and I agreed.

OCTOBER 17

Tuesday at group was disaster.

OCTOBER 18

Gail said she does care about me and I do matter.

OCTOBER 21

Yesterday in group, I mentioned how this last week Eugene makes my skin crawl and I want to scream within five minutes of being around him, even though we've spent so little time together. He also seems to be walking in my brother's shadow. Gail expressed her concern about it today. She suggested it was my body's way of telling me that at this point promising Eugene we could stay together for another month was too much. She brought up the subject of medication again. She feels I'm too stressed out.

$$\overline{V}$$

A Haven

Losing my job was a relief. I was freed from my nasty boss, the long commute, and too much work, but came under increased financial pressure, trying to divvy up a pittance among various creditors. Eugene wouldn't help with the bills or household chores. He spent money. He watched t.v. When I felt good, he slapped me with doom and gloom until I was miserable again. When I felt bad, he got angry. I stayed away from home as much as I could. I wasn't sleeping. I worried. I struggled with memories and feelings that terrified me.

Gail had begun to suggest medication, at least sleeping pills, because of the stress I was under. I refused. I knew people for whom medication was helpful. I knew they weren't crazy. But when it came to myself, I could only consider medication from my family's view-point: proof that I was insane and could be dismissed. I saw it as defeat, caving in to their view of me, after I'd fought so hard to believe in my reality.

Finally I realized that I couldn't cope much longer. Because my marriage was by far the greatest cause of stress in my life, everything else I did to reduce my stress had only a slight effect. If I stayed with Eugene, I was going to end up on medication. At best. From there it was anyone's guess. I felt I had to choose between Eugene and my sanity. I wasn't ready to admit that Eugene was abusive and I deserved better. That would mean feeling my anger and hurt at his abuse, forgiving myself for enduring it, and accepting my innocence and my right to be cherished. All more than I could do. But I could act on the messages I drew unconsciously from dreams, songs and stories like "Bontsha the Silent," through which I told myself I was oppressed and needn't be. I had support in my life. I had developed some

43

strength and self-esteem. When pressed to the wall I was now able to jump over it.

On October 21 I asked Eugene to leave for two weeks, ostensibly because I needed some time to myself. I tried to be reassuring about our relationship. I thought if I were honest about wanting to split up, he would ask me not to and I was afraid I might give in.

Eugene called a few days later about making the separation permanent. I immediately packed up all his things and stuck them away in the back of a closet. I didn't realize Eugene was trying to use his old tricks to bring me to heel, but I was no longer susceptible. I didn't feel threatened by his attempt to abandon me. I was thrilled.

* * * * *

OCTOBER 22

Eugene called today. His voice seemed to be from far off, like a bad memory returning, reverberating with echoes of my brother.

OCTOBER 30

All the wonderful and good things happening lately! I washed the bathroom tiles today. They sparkle. I'm going to do the bathroom in white and yellow. It's a beautiful, sunny day. I've been opening and dealing with the mail since Eugene left. I've brought most of the bills up to date. The apartment is tidy and almost clean. I still have to defrost the freezer and clean out all the cupboards, but counters, wall, floors are wonderfully, shiny, clean! I went swimming this morning, though I just had ten minutes to spare. At one time I wouldn't have done that. I'm not coughing any more. I can smell something besides tobacco in the apartment. I enjoy being at home with the cats. It feels like a haven. Ann says I sound like a different person. I'm sleeping. I'm planning how and when to redecorate the apartment, given limited time and money. It's fun to plan. I'm still working on my vase in the pottery class. On Friday I drove through the countryside taking photographs.

I feel more whole than I've felt in a long, long time.

NOVEMBER 3

I called Ellen last night. She's starting with a new firm on Monday and is very happy about it. I talked to her about my work, plans to redecorate the apartment, etc. I enjoyed talking to her. She said she'd call next week.

NOVEMBER 6

I invited Mary for lunch. I had fun preparing the meal and having a friend over. It wasn't a comfortable thing to do before.

NOVEMBER 9

New buds are blooming on my gloxinia. Gail said I could write about my feelings twice a week.

I'm sad for wanting so little. I've needed comfort so badly and thought a man would provide it. I'm scared too, now that the first flush of exhilaration is past. I suppose it's like everything I do for myself, terrifying until I get used to it. Separation is such a bigger, more positive step, it's a wonder I'm not totally petrified. It's sad too. It's an ending and a beginning.

Lately it seems that even when I feel bad, there's some irrepressible joy in me that keeps bubbling to the surface.

NOVEMBER 13

I told Ann about Gail going on holiday over Christmas. She said she'd be there for me to talk to. That made me feel really good.

NOVEMBER 15

Eugene called to ask me out. I said no.

NOVEMBER 16

The new chalk pastels I bought flow onto paper like paint.

What a lovely, lazy day. I'm having a bath, thinking about putting on my clean pyjamas and getting into a freshly made bed. The apartment gives me such pleasure. It's home. I've never had that feeling before, a feeling of place.

My friends are good to me. Life is good to me. The excitement and wonder of it!

NOVEMBER 18

Eugene has been calling every other day to tell me how much he loves me and how distraught he is. Every night I dream that I have no right to separate from him.

NOVEMBER 19

I'm in pottery class, waiting for my slabs to dry. I like working with clay, it has a life of its own. You're never absolutely sure what will turn out.

I have to find some way of setting limits with Ruth. I like her a lot but she asks too much. She expects to talk every night for a couple of hours. I'm afraid to say that I want to get off the phone because it offends her. She expects me to see her at least once a week. She says she doesn't open up easily, but opens up to me. I feel as though somehow I've convinced her to trust me, caused her to be vulnerable, and I must not betray that trust at any cost.

NOVEMBER 20

I'm looking out the window at a night made bright by light reflected off snow, a soft blanket on the evergreens and the roof top below, so peaceful, a gift from God.

NOVEMBER 21

Wisdom from Ann: it's better to lose a friend than lose your mind.

NOVEMBER 22

Speaking to Ruth this morning I tried, in my clumsy way, to be honest about wanting to spend less time on the phone. She said she wished she hadn't opened up to me, was right in not trusting people, would never trust anyone again, would withdraw. She's called five or six times since then. She says she's shivering and her stomach hurts. She can't keep anything down. She feels like dying. I wonder if what I've done is so very wrong.

NOVEMBER 27

I'm sitting on the window ledge. Snowball came up to join me, stretching full-length against the window, up on his hind legs, mewing at the outside. The flickering lights of an airplane cross the night sky. There is a place of safety for me, but I can't, I just can't get inside yet. Someday I will. I've had my warm milk and cookies. It's time for bed.

NOVEMBER 29

I met Eugene at a coffee shop to bring him the rest of his clothes. I felt unreal. I saw him as a stranger — was this the man I'd lived with for almost ten years?

DECEMBER 2

I slept over at Ann's last night. Rob was out of town. I played with the baby while Ann did some work. Then I brought her books up to date and gave her some direction about the year-end. She thanked me a million times. I don't know what for.

DECEMBER 4

Gail says I'm drained because I don't accept what people give me. But if I accept that people give to me for who I am, if I accept comfort from my friends, I must feel the terrible sadness and comfortlessness of my childhood. There was no one to turn to, no one to rely on or protect me. I'd have to face the crushing burden of that independence if I stopped viewing it as an axiom of my life.

DECEMBER 9

I'm sitting on the window ledge, waiting for the pledge break on PBS to be over. The night is beautiful, the apartment finally warm now that the furnace is working, heat curling up from the radiator around my feet. Sometimes it feels as if I'm slogging through a never-ending swamp. But you know what? Even just to be able to write again, makes the yuck of therapy worth it. There's something in me that must write. It was shoved away in a shadowy corner of shame. Now it is in the light, growing. I will get to the other side.

DECEMBER 12

I'm sick of trying to be patient. I'm not patient. I want to get it over with. I don't want to be reasonable and realize that letting everything out at once would drive me crazy. I don't want to remember that I've felt bad before and it didn't last forever. It feels as if it's going to last forever.

DECEMBER 13

Joy returns. How wonderful to be in my home. My home! What a word "home" is: my own place, with my music and the cats playing, kettle on to boil, sitting on the window ledge, warmth at my feet and frost against my arm as I look out on the great world of the night, my lamp reflected against the mist of my breath on the window pane. What a rambling sentence. What a warm, rambling feeling.

DECEMBER 15

I'm going to burst. What am I excited about, you ask? Well, I'll tell you. I'm going to be teaching a full course at the university come January!

DECEMBER 20

I'm so frustrated. I'm pulling as hard as I'm able, but can't wrench my mind off certain tracks.

DECEMBER 23

Although I give and give, it never seems enough to compensate for the badness within me. My parents abandoned me because I was awful. That's why my brother molested me. My badness was a poison that seeped out and tainted the family.

My face is burning. My head hurts. I'm scared.

Surely my friends, who are sweet to me, must be angels from heaven to embrace the shit my parents rejected.

DECEMBER 25

Ruth and I had a doozy of a fight because I wanted to get off the phone after talking for two hours. I feel bad because she's such a good friend when I'm in trouble, but she wants so much from me.

1987

JANUARY 1

A brand new year, anything can happen. I had fun with friends last night. We went out for dinner, came back here and listened to music, talked until early morning. Ruth left a half hour of messages on my tape about how hurt and rejected she feels.

JANUARY 2

Laying in bed, my mind drifting, I suddenly thought, "I wonder if I'm replacing Eugene with Ruth." I'm messing up my happiness, stressed out because of the energy her hurts, her possessiveness, her touchiness demand. I'm aghast. I care for her. I don't want to hurt her. What am I to do? She wants me to fill all her emotional needs. She's jealous of my time with other people. I never know what will trigger a barrage.

JANUARY 4

I've had the loveliest weekend, doing all the alone kinds of things I like to do.

JANUARY 6

I spoke to Ruth, told her that I only want to talk once a week. I don't want to discuss feelings, and I don't want to get together for the time being.

JANUARY 7

Sometimes it's hard to keep in mind the good things. And yet, someday my soul will be completely unfolded in its full and natural self. The shadows, the unknown memories and feelings that scare me out of my wits and cause me to act in self-destructive ways, will diminish in the bright light of day. The ice in my heart will be melted.

JANUARY 8
Who am I? A scary question, a sad question. It makes me want to cry.

JANUARY 13
A nightmare last night: I couldn't get Eugene to leave. Finally he did. I locked the door. The lock began to buckle and the door opened slowly. It was my brother.

I can give up the legacy of guilt at a price. The price is losing numbness, and feeling my feelings.

JANUARY 14
It hurts to think of the little kid I was, so alone and defenseless. I wanted to die. I felt dirty. I felt used. My parents gave me many good things, but not safety. They looked the other way, full of empty words and kisses.

JANUARY 16
Gail talked about my going back to group. Too scary. I'm not ready now. Maybe spring or fall.

I feel as though Gail has dominion over me. She lays down the law, though I can petition her rulings. I feel like a supplicant to the court of the king.

I'm having a tough time with this dominion-dependency thing. I could view things differently, look at it as a helping, nurturing relationship. But that hasn't been my experience. My experience as a dependent was one of betrayal. I tried to be left alone as much as possible. I don't know how to feel any differently. Maybe it requires a leap of faith.

JANUARY 20

I am so excited. The doldrums are gone. I feel as though I'm trembling on the edge — the edge of discovery or the edge of a cliff? It's frightening. It's thrilling. The danger is worth the chance to fly free. There is so much so see and do and feel!! Did one of the bars to the cage around my heart spring open today? Winter is a time for replenishment and reflection before the great burst of spring. Winter beauty is peaceful, God's lullaby to the troubled mind. I can rest in the view from my window.

JANUARY 22

If I am not a receptacle for the wishes of the dead and not a receptacle for my brother's sex, then what am I?

There was a time I was numb and unaware. Now I am less numb and more aware. There's room for joy and pain. On a winter's night, I look at distant lights and tears come to my eyes. What a marvelous thing to be able to cry.

JANUARY 24

Last night I dreamt that a religious Jew was trying to rape me.

JANUARY 25

Ellen and her husband were in town, visiting friends. She stopped over and we talked for three and a half hours. I'm really happy about it. I wonder if I said too much, but I just responded to her questions. Ellen's comments about our childhood:

There was power in my moods, anger and hostility. I gave looks that could kill. I said little, but they were zingers when I did and the family tiptoed around me. Ted was Mama's pet, a real pet, like a dog, say. Mama was *farbinden* (tied up) with Ted. Their relationship was twisted. If anybody, Mama would be the one who abused him. Ellen said that she was Mum and Dad's child. Ted was Mama's. I was Dad's. I told her that I felt as though I had to take care of Dad. Ellen then said that I was nobody's child. She said that Mum and Dad were willing to act differently with her because they were so relieved that she wasn't like me.

JANUARY 27

There's a side to Mum that's like me. I remember her laughing and howling at the wind on a bright, moonlit night.

JANUARY 29

Ellen told me Ted keeps getting more uptight about religion. He's always extremely tense if religious observance isn't done correctly to the letter. Does he think God will strike him dead if he does it wrong? How sad.

FEBRUARY 3

Part of me screams with the desire to communicate, but is strangled by another part of me so that the scream is utterly silent. The intensity of that silent communication demands to be heard, but who can hear silence? Is it that way for Dad, the other silent one in the family?

FEBRUARY 5

Ruth left a message on my machine. She's not talking to me any more.

FEBRUARY 8

I've been thinking about Ruth and the similar relationships I've had. Why have I continued to work so hard at them when they make me feel bad? (Snowball is at the window, patting the glass. He looks like he's trying to catch a snowflake.) The intensity makes me feel real, as if I matter. It makes me feel important, cared about, listened to. But the irony is that each of these people has in some fundamental way operated on a totally different wavelength from me, so that I really wasn't heard at all. Now isn't that strange?

$$\overline{\text{VI}}$$

Innocent

It wasn't unusual that I worked hard at maintaining destructive relationships. They were what I knew as "normal." When I could recognize that they made me feel bad, it was a terrific change. I was learning from Gail, both as a teacher and as a living, caring example, how it felt to be nurtured and how that differed from what I'd experienced in my family and marriage. The shock of coming so close to cracking made me aware that I had a limited amount of energy, which was drained by the negative elements in my life and renewed by the positive. Gail taught me how to build up the positive side — by my outlook, by balancing work and play, by the people I chose to be with. Once I got rid of Eugene, all the energy tied up in surviving his abuse was suddenly freed. I could use it to deal with my past and go on to feel, change, grow, and risk.

As a child stuck in an abusive home, surviving was the best I could do. As an adult, survival consumed me. It takes a lot of energy to suppress feelings, to act parts, to cope with adult responsibilities. Not knowing how to care for myself or allow others to care for me, I couldn't replenish myself. Abuse depleted me further, an easy target because it seemed normal.

Distractions like worrying, food, work, drugs and relationships push away discomforting feelings. Survivors use these distractions to feel better, but instead they bring pain and shame. The more tired we become, the more we sacrifice to keep going. We get weaker, becoming more susceptible to abuse. We sacrifice more, feeling worse, look for more distraction, which depletes us further. It is a desperate, contracting spiral. Sometimes surviving feels like death.

In recovering, I reversed the spiral. It began with simple contact between me and Gail, the experience of her care breaking the cycle

53

of sacrifice and depletion. I learned about alternatives to my childhood relationships, let go of distraction, and stopped using up so much energy in suppressing myself. I began to be relieved of old anger and hurt, took some of that freed up energy and got out of danger. I found new pleasures, had more energy to feel, to remember the good and bad, to take in caring, to chance new ways of being, to be joyous. I felt better about myself and found innocence.

There were times I wasn't comfortable with hope and possibility. I had been trapped in abusive situations for much of my life. I was accustomed to the gloom of Eugene and my family. A part of me preferred the safety of the known, as horrible as it was, to the risky business of becoming myself. The lessons of survival that had served me so well — being quiet, faking it, compliance — were hard to let go for the unproven rewards of being me. I struggled with myself. The whole part of me used my best skills to help me go on. The part of me that was scared used my best skills to hold me back.

Gail's job was to point out the traps I fell into, showing me how to get out. When I focused on my weaknesses, she brought up my strengths. When I set up impossible expectations, she helped me tone them down. When I drew pictures of storm clouds, she reminded me that clouds bring rain, and rain makes the plants grow. It pissed me off. But it spurred me to positive action. Bit by bit, the whole part of me got bigger, encompassing the scared little girl, growing up.

*   *   *   *   *

FEBRUARY 14

A dream, just before I woke this morning: Gail had a magnifying glass. She focused it on her hand, saying, "Look at this. It's amazing the things you see when you look through this glass and then look at my face." I was really concentrating on the glass. When Gail said, "look at my face," she moved the glass away and I looked at her face. I saw Mama. I shut my eyes and shouted, "It's her. She did it. I know. She did it." I started screaming and crying. Gail put her arms around me and whispered, "Remember there are other people here." I cried quietly, holding onto Gail for dear life.

The sun is sparkling through my window. It looks like fairy dust. I feel good, lighter in my heart.

FEBRUARY 15

I woke up at 7:15 to see the full moon shining and a haze of pink just over the horizon. I'm tired. I've been working too hard again. I think I'll take today off and do a lot of pleasant things. There. I can breathe easier.

I used to accept being hugged so I could hug my friends. Now, I draw warmth from being hugged. I'm not afraid of it any more.

FEBRUARY 20

I hate being angry. It's so uncomfortable because I don't do anything with it. Pardon — I do something, indeed. I paste the offence into my scrapbook of "Things X Has Done to Piss Me Off." My anger and discomfort grow along with the scrapbook. I feel at such a loss with anger. Expressing it scares me. Not expressing anger leaves me feeling awful, still mad and a failure to boot.

I'm so frustrated I could scream. Oh, I'll do all the "right" things. I hit the couch. I'll go swimming or running. I told my friends I'm in a pissy mood. I don't care. I'm tired of being strangled by fear. I'm tired of my head hurting, of being anxious. I am tired of hiding from myself.

FEBRUARY 21

If I keep blocking myself, will Gail help me or give up on me?

I've asked Gail if she'll kick me out of therapy because of the blocks and she said no. But I still want to ask her again. I'm afraid that she is going to realize I'm really crazy and will abandon me. I'm angry at her for stripping away the techniques I use to stop myself.

FEBRUARY 25

I am so thrilled to actually own something. I have savings! Ann left a message on my machine for "the lady of the assets."

MARCH 1

I had an awful nightmare last night. I woke up feeling as though I was going to vomit. I lay quite still until the feeling passed.

The dream started off with me as an adult, coming on to someone. I was inviting him out and I had sexual feelings toward him. There was a house in the distance. Then I was in the house and I was a child. There were two evils in the house, a greater evil and a lesser evil. Children were kept separate from their parents, but I was with my parents. My sister was on the floor below us, above the garage. Children wrote poetry to describe what was really going on, but the two evils took it away and kept it for themselves. Some great poetry was lost to the world.

MARCH 10

My voice is the part of me that wants to be whole.

MARCH 13

I'm so happy, I could burst! Dear God, how wonderful it is to be alive. The plants and the cats and I are thriving. Only two more pages to this notebook. The next notebook brings in spring. Beautiful winter trees will burst forth — and what else? Who knows. Anything can happen in a blank notebook.

MARCH 17

I just got a letter from Mum. She wrote, "Enclosed is a gift for you for Passover. Get yourself something special just like you are very special." I burst into tears. I've wanted so much to hear that, to be able to hear it.

Mum and Dad have agreed to see Gail with me during the week of May 13. That's fine.

MARCH 19

I had six nightmares last night, one an hour. The worst one was at 6:00. I dreamt I was married to someone crazy.

MARCH 23

My renewed interest in clothes comes from the loosening of a tight knot: "I'm horribly ugly" — translate: "very bad, it's all my fault." Associated with that wonderful feeling of coming alive is my pain and anger over the incest. I tried to fend off those thoughts and feelings over the last few days, but an anxiety attack hit me in the stomach this afternoon. When I realized how angry I was, I hit the couch with a hanger and then I danced. After that I wasn't anxious any more. I was flying. I tried on every top I own with my new skirt and finally went to bed around 1:00 a.m. That's a big change: from the beginning of my anxiety attack to the dissipation of my anger (for the time being), only three and a half hours.

Dawn is coming. The sky is blue now, so many beautiful shades of blue.

MARCH 24

It makes me sick to think of being little and being touched, touching, naked. All the good things, being more whole, clothes, cats, friends — I can't feel them now. All I can feel is shortness of breath, a burst of pain and tears, then nothing. I can't open myself to joy. The hurt is too close to the surface and I can only take it a bit at a time.

MARCH 26

I had an interesting dream last night: I was writing a story about incest, titled "Scrambled Eggs." I asked myself, in the dream, why the story was called "Scrambled Eggs." I answered, "because once my life was sunny-side up and then it became scrambled." I think that's a good description.

I hate my brother. I can't bear to use his name. I hate him!

MARCH 27

Why do I cling to my position of notoriety in the family? It's a position of some power and control. If I give that up, I have to face my vulnerability. It means facing the fact that I was a child. And it hurts so much to feel the desperation and helplessness of my childhood.

MARCH 29

It's more pleasant to be sad in a freshly vacuumed room. The croton looks beautiful between the computer table and the stereo, below "American Landscapes."

MARCH 31

How lovely! The iced trees look like something out of fairyland. The snow is a falling mist — quiet, quiet. Snowball came over to sit on my feet, so warm and soft.

Gail says if I accept fully that I was a child and the incest wasn't my fault, I have to grow up. Interesting.

APRIL 3

It's hard to think of myself as good and bad, not something in capital letters, not VICTIM or SUPERWOMAN.

APRIL 10

Dear Mum and Dad:

I want to wish you a wonderful Passover. I love Passover. Some of my most treasured memories are of Dad reading the Haggadah.[1] It wasn't his tune or the fluidity of his reading that was so wonderful, but the way it seemed to come from his soul. When Dad read "I lead you out of the land of Egypt, I myself, *Ani vi lo saraph, Ani vi lo Malakh* (I and not an angel, I and not a messenger)," I had a picture of Dad being ten feet tall with a long white beard, standing and pointing his finger. Dad explained the Haggadah, and I understood when he said that we ourselves were led from the land of Egypt. Dad always told us how Pesakh (Passover) had special meaning for him, because he really was a slave in the concentration camp and was liberated. To me, Passover is a celebration of freedom. For each person it has a special meaning that is his or hers alone, and yet can be shared and experienced by all. You created an atmosphere of wonder and miracles that made me believe anything was possible on

---

1 Haggadah means "The Telling," and is the story of the exodus from Egypt, which is read and sung on the eve of Passover.

this night so very different from any other. You gave me a precious gift, a feeling of continuity with thousands of years of history, a feeling of immediacy in the meaning of freedom in my own life, compassion for the stranger in a strange land, the beauty of the holiday in springtime surrounded by blooming flowers, belief in the "anything can happen-ness" of life, and a wonderful pure joy at being alive.

Thank you.

APRIL 13

How lucky I am to be alive on this glorious day, to be me here in this place and time! Can you believe it? Me, saying I'm happy to be *me, here, now*???!!

APRIL 15

How can I deal with such a mixture of feelings: appreciation and love for Mum and Dad, resentment, anger.

What Ted did to me wasn't so bad.

But it was violation. Gail called it evil. It felt like an assault. This is hard.

I was innocent.

I was innocent. I was a child and now I'm grown up. At the core of my being is a pure soul, the innocence of childhood.

As a child, alone in a terrible situation, crying for the love around me to ease that terribleness, I was left to deal with it on my own. In the incomprehensibility of being forsaken, I felt my soul to be wicked, unforgivable, unanswerable, torn apart.

I am innocent. Can I deal with that?

TWO

Middle

VII

Cold Where the Universe Ends

We who were abused as children by our families blamed ourselves. Whether or not we were told that we caused the abuse, we assumed responsibility, not knowing that people act on their own impulses and outside our control. Because we missed the nurturing we needed to grow up, we continue to see ourselves as cause and centre, carrying with us guilt for the uncaring actions of our family. We believe that if we were better, we could make them care.

I tried to make the people in my life care by doing what they expected of me. But they continued to hurt me and I believed that it was my fault. In therapy I began to learn that I had no control over other people's actions or feelings. I couldn't fix them. I could only fix myself. As I redirected my efforts from controlling others to developing myself, I was excited by the potential to honour my feelings, dreams, values, desires, and abilities. I was also scared. Realizing my potential meant exposing my true self to unknown reactions, relinquishing the outer self, which had enabled me to survive the destructive responses of my family and husband. Change was possible only when I believed that my true self could slowly emerge in surroundings that were safe.

Safety is a matter of fact. Some situations endangered my physical or emotional health. Because I was used to being used and abused, it felt normal. To be safe, I had to learn to recognize, avoid and extricate myself from danger.

Safety is also a matter of degree. Some situations are safe for one activity and not another, safe for a certain amount of intimacy, but not a greater amount. Used to all or nothing, I had to learn how to be discriminating.

Finally, safety depends on feeling safe. It was hard to believe that I was, at last, out of danger. I was always looking over my shoulder, waiting for the unexpected blow. As I developed trust in myself and the trustworthy people in my life, I felt more secure and could reveal more of myself.

My sense of safety started with Gail and grew over time as I noticed the honest, caring and direct way in which she consistently treated me. I could depend on her and little by little I did, though her reliability was painful because it was such a contrast to the betrayal I experienced at home.

✓ By taking on responsibility for my family's behaviour, I dulled my reaction to their betrayal. I felt guilt instead of anger and hurt. I felt guilt instead of suffering the profound, irretrievable loss of childhood. Letting go of guilt was a dual process: learning that I was not responsible for my family, and developing the emotional equipment to handle my anger, hurt and loss.

With the discovery of my innocence, I thought I had finished blaming myself for my feelings, for other people's feelings, for their actions and reactions. But guilt resurged whenever I started a new stage of healing. Each time, letting go of guilt was a critical step in the process of facing the past and of making my future different. Each time, removing the mask of guilt revealed some aspect of myself I never lost again. When I gave up guilt for my brother's abuse, I began to believe that, at bottom, I was a good person.

1987

APRIL 16

It was so terribly hard to say to Gail that I am innocent of the incest. The sky is beautiful tonight: washes of white on blue, sun setting in a pool of rose behind tree tops and birds. I'm teetering between anxiety and excitement. I cry over Pesakh because of what it means to me. I feel free. For so many years, I felt trapped and smothered.

Who am I? Sitting at the table with my cats, Mitzi licking my fingers, Snowball cuddled against me, who am I?

APRIL 18

"Hi Darling. We got your letter, *maidele* (little girl), and we both were really touched. I had tears in my eyes. I wasn't aware that our Pesakh impressed you so much. But anyhow ..."

That was the message from Dad I came home to. Isn't that lovely? But you know, I have told both Mum and Dad before how I feel about Passover. I wonder why they couldn't hear me.

APRIL 20

I keep telling myself that I'm never going to get a notarized affidavit detailing the incest. I have to trust myself. The alternative is to doubt my sanity, something I've done for too long and that's got me nowhere. Belief in my sanity, in my right to be, has got me everywhere.

I'm glad there were several pieces in *Voices In The Night*[1] about brother-sister incest. Most of the literature glosses over it, and I feel as if I have no right to pain and anger. Reading those pieces made me believe that I have the right to my feelings.

APRIL 21

COLD WHERE THE UNIVERSE ENDS

I often dream that I'm in a play but I've forgotten my lines, or I don't know what part I'm playing, or half way through a speech I realize I never read the script. I panic, confused, because I suddenly don't know what's happening around me. The situation is vaguely familiar, my presence accepted by the other actors. They seem to know what's going on, but I don't.

For me, being an incest survivor is like that dream. My memories often feel unconnected to me, as if I'm remembering characters acting

---

1 Toni A. H. McNaron and Yarrow Morgan, eds., *Voices In the Night, Women Speaking About Incest* (San Francisco: Cleis Press, 1982).

on a stage, but I can't remember the whole play. I'm afraid to acknowledge the reality of my memories. Would I be overwhelmed by the pain of being that little girl? It's so much easier to watch from the safety of the audience, believing that the house lights will go up, and we'll all go home.

My family was special. We were better than everyone else, but to preserve that special quality we couldn't talk to anyone outside the family about personal matters. It was hard for me to figure out what was personal. Sometimes the brand of detergent we used was personal. It was safer to say nothing and just walk around smug in the secret knowledge of our superiority. Our intelligence, sensitivity and morality didn't seem to fit with a brother who abused me. Not that I gave it any thought. I couldn't. It would shatter my world. But at night, in the quiet of the dark, my part played for the day, I'd feel as if I were going to die. Though I twisted and turned, I could find no way out. I felt as if the life were being squeezed out of me. I couldn't breathe. The incongruity couldn't be resolved. Escape from my brother was impossible. It couldn't be happening. It just couldn't. But it was. The "couldn't be's" and "but it is" made me feel crazy, and only the thought that "nothing matters, nothing is real, nothing exists," brought me peace.

The year that I was eleven, I started to sleep with my doll again. I talked to her, thinking and whispering while my little sister slept across from me, six years younger and too old for dolls. "Snow White," I'd whisper, "I wish you were real. I wish you could answer me. But you're not real. There's no one to answer but me. You're just me. But oh, Snow White, I don't want to die. When you die there's nothing. Can you imagine nothing? Nothing to see, nothing to hear, nothing to feel." Night after night, I'd cry myself to sleep, picturing nothingness. Night after night, I'd wake up, screaming. Until eventually, my terrible fear of nothingness became a crooning lullaby, "nothing matters, nothing is real, nothing exists." I'd still wake up screaming, but my tears had frozen. I lived my waking life in absolute zero, the temperature at which molecules stop moving.

There were times when I was married that my numbness started to crack. I'd lie in bed, crying quietly so as not to wake my husband.

I'd feel smothered. I could see no way out, as if I were going to die. I'd whisper to myself, "nothing matters, nothing is real, nothing exists," and fall asleep, my numbness restored. I was oblivious to the familiarity of the situation.

My brother was smart. Six years older than me, he was grown up, awesome in his goodness. He graduated from high school with top honours. I was bursting with pride for him. He was also sexually abusing me, but that was not in the waking daytime world of my family. That occurred somewhere else.

The first time I was ten. He was babysitting and I did something wrong, so he spanked me. My sister sat on my bed, watching. He sat on my grandmother's bed and put me over his lap. Then he sent me to the bathroom to wait for him. He was going to show me something. I was glad he'd stopped spanking me. I waited for what seemed an endless time, afraid to leave the bathroom, until he came back and told me that he'd wanted to show me something about having babies, but it hadn't worked. He had another idea, though. The memory stops there, but it's enough to show that the abuse was my fault. After all, I'd done something wrong. I got spanked for it and then had to make up for it.

When I first separated from my husband, I wondered how I stood for his calling me a "dirty bitch" while we made love or screaming at me in the middle of the street, "castrating cunt." I thought of myself as an independent woman, a feminist, not one of those poor, weak-willed women who allow themselves to be beaten. How I longed for a punch. Just one fist to my eye. I'd never stand for that, I thought. I could walk out then. So I imagined.

Once on my own, I looked back at the degradation I accepted, and wondered who that woman was. The day I remembered my brother calling me a cunt and a bitch while he used me, I realized how much it reminded me of the way my husband treated me. The woman who was an independent feminist lost her scorn for the woman who hung her head while she was humiliated in public.

Alongside the feminist and the woman who hung her head in shame is the little girl who lived in the cold where the universe ends: beyond the clash of family myth and terrible reality, beyond the fear and pain of being abused, beyond shame and humiliation and guilt, far beyond rage. There was no place for me at home. There was no place for me in the world. In absolute zero, I could be numb. In that place where complete betrayal would not affect me, the end of the line, in the cold where the universe ends, I could survive.

Now, walking back into the world, I burn with awakening feelings and new found memories that once I was certain were frozen forever.

It was terrible to remember that my brother tried to penetrate me, his disgust when I cried out in pain, his disgruntled acceptance of a hand job, my bewildered sense of failure and shame.

It was terrible to remember being smothered, his heavy breathing making me sick, the whiteness of his skin like something dead on top of me.

It is terrible to realize that this happened to me. I was that hurt, lonely, scared little girl, not some character on a stage.

All through my life, my perceptions ran smack into the wall of someone else's certainty. My family and my husband knew me better than I knew myself. I retreated from their rightness, from the madness of "I'm wrong, I'm wrong," and "But I saw, I heard, I felt" to the end of the universe.

I'm walking back now. I have a place in the world, though the road is long and hard. It winds through mountains, bog, thorny thickets. And through green meadows and moonlit nights. There are people walking beside me, who support me when I limp, hug me when I make it through the swamp, and share my joy in a soft breeze and sunshine.

VIII

Dear Mum and Dad

"Cold Where the Universe Ends" was my first purely autobiographical story. It stunned me with its power to reveal myself to me, and with the impact it had on those who read it. I realized that writing openly about my experiences was meaningful to other people and vital to my self-discovery. For the first time I saw myself as a victim and felt the painful reality of being sexually abused by my brother. Losing the view of myself as a tower of independence and strength was distressing. But in giving up some illusions and accepting myself as a victim, I discovered the real strengths of my survivorship. I found belief in myself and my ability to make my life my own. A belief I had struggled toward for many years.

Abuse in the home is enabled by deception. The truth is dangerous to abusers, who might be punished, or at least stopped. The family which is used to operating with abuse runs the risk of change if the abuse becomes known. By guarding the family secrets, deception protects the abuser from discovery and the family from change.

Despite the lies and the silence, my true self maintained a voice through the exercise of my imagination — in dreams, fantasy, make-believe games, and stories. From childhood to adulthood I unconsciously told the truth in symbols, which allowed me to express my feelings without revealing the family secrets.

As a child, I invented make-believe games to act out my experiences. My grandmother became the wicked witch who captured and tormented me and my friends. My brother became the master who forced us to do hateful, impossible deeds, while demanding demonstrations of affection. I could safely describe my situation and express my feelings through the use of these symbols, because the family deception wasn't threatened by it. My family didn't recognize the truth in my symbols. On the contrary, they saw my imagination as symptomatic of craziness. It was proof that I was up in the clouds somewhere, with a loose grip on reality.

Writing gave my imagination a permanent existence on paper though I continued, unknowingly, to disguise the truth with fiction. Writing was a powerful way for me to express and explore my reality, but I had little control over what came out in the process. Sometimes, unable to tolerate even disguised truth, my imagination locked shut. I didn't understand why. I hated myself when I couldn't write. Losing touch with my inner self, I was engulfed by the family deception, believing I was lazy and useless. I liked to read my stories to my parents because it was a way to make contact as my true self. They responded positively, especially my mother. It was a peculiar kind of contact, telling truths they couldn't face, reinforcing their view of my dreaminess. Yet, it allowed me to share real thoughts and feelings that I could not reveal any other way. After my brother left home, I felt safer. With this greater security, my stories grew less disguised. I could no longer share them with my parents, and lost the one way in which I'd been able to relate to them honestly.

Periodically I wrote in a journal, facing the same issues I discovered in therapy years later. At fifteen, I wrote:

I find myself yearning for that which I don't as yet know how to make possible. I go in my dreams where I cannot go in reality.

At sixteen:

Sometimes I feel how beautiful life is, what a gift to us. But at other times I am overwhelmed by loneliness, sadness, depression.

At seventeen:

Little by little, I'm dying inside. Where's the evil dragon I'm to fight? It doesn't exist — only a vague amorphous collection of memories that insist the formula for fulfilment lies in conformity. There's only me. I've got to change. I have to win every round

— against myself. If I lose, I lose part of what I am. There's only me.

On my eighteenth birthday:

> Sometimes I think I'm just holding on by my teeth. I get really scared. I'm afraid of loneliness, afraid of becoming a dull drudge. I want to cry. Often in the evenings, I am sad, wondering what's to become of me. I believe I can't write. I'm useless. I feel nonexistent. I prefer to think of myself as being unique. This uniqueness declares me to be me, gives me power in a nightmare world. I've never felt so powerless, so helpless, as now, feeling myself to have common problems and thoughts. Still, I can never truly believe in my depths that I'm not different.

My journal writing never lasted long. I wasn't able to deal with the truth because, being at home, I was still open to the dangers that telling the truth brought in my family. After I left home, moving to another city, my stories began to focus less on school and friends, and more on my family life. They uncovered my true self to a much greater depth than before, and again I faced the dilemma provoked by my earlier journals. How could I contain these intense feelings and thoughts when I didn't understand where they came from and didn't have the tools or support to deal with them? I wrote to a friend from university:

> No matter what happens, you can't not dance. You have to pretend life, make believe joy. Who am I in this room of my own making, this protective island, a self-made jail? It's an obscene question isn't it? Especially tasteless because it hurts to even try and answer a question like that. Why am I so sad? I am listening to the radio and feel like letting the tears just stream down my cheeks. I won't, of course, because then I might cry forever. I don't know why I feel as though I could sit forever at my desk and just stare out at the city's lights. I am nuts, bonkers, out of

my head, and so I wish that I were dead. I don't really wish that but it rhymed so neatly.

My freedom was growing because I'd left home and was writing. As my inner self emerged, I again felt the pain that I'd spent most of my life blocking. I tried the counselling centre at school. The counsellor didn't encourage me to discover my feelings and desires. Instead, she told me about hers. I was good at being what someone else wanted me to be, I'd learned it at home and practised all my life. Without knowing it, I absorbed the counsellor's messages and fed them back to her. She was mightily impressed by my "improvement." I gave in to depression and found Eugene.

I was interested in Eugene because he was interested in writing. I showed him my work and he encouraged me. But his encouragement was a terrible deception. Under Eugene's domination I could not tolerate the pain my writing would reveal, nor would he permit the integrity of my writing. He forced me to throw out the work that was most revealing of my family. In doing that I threw out part of myself. I think he recognized the power in my writing and tried to control it. Rather than let him twist my writing as he twisted everything else, I gave it up. It was as if I relinquished my last hold on the living world, entering the land of the dead.

I believed I'd lost my ability to write, losing myself. In fact, I'd stopped writing to protect the core of my true self from Eugene's violation. When I started therapy, I was strong enough to face what writing would reveal and to resist any attempts Eugene might make to control it. I knew I would never again allow myself to be separated from the part of me that writes.

Even though I had been living away from home for many years, I carried with me the family view. I was still tentative about the truth I was discovering, so different from the deception my family shared. I wasn't strong enough to sustain my perspective when it came into conflict with theirs. In order to continue the exploration of my reality, I had to cut off contact with my parents for some time. I didn't make a conscious decision at first, but somehow they got the message and stopped calling. My father wrote me an honest, direct letter that surprised me because my family doesn't go in for honesty and directness. I was deeply touched by his concern and respect for how I wanted to handle the relationship. I wrote back that I preferred not to speak for a while and would let them know when I was ready to communicate by letter. After a few months I did. For several more months we corresponded. I loved writing and getting letters from them. We seemed to relate better on paper than we had ever been able to when we talked. I hoped this improved relationship via correspondence would lead to an improved face to face relationship. I tried to be reasonable, knowing my parents might never change enough to accept me as I really was. Still I hoped that one day they would give me the affirmation I hadn't received from them as a child.

With Passover approaching, I was filled with the beautiful memories of our *seders*,[1] and the hope of sharing a larger part of my life with my parents. I wanted to call them but was hesitant because we hadn't spoken for so long. I thought it might be better to wait until we saw each other in May. As if she was reading my thoughts, my mother phoned just before Passover. I was thrilled. I felt enough self-confidence to start talking to them, warmed and encouraged by our letters. We discussed the meeting we were to have with Gail, an information-gathering session in May. My father was planning to be in town for a convention then and my mother would come with him. I was excited because, for the first time since I left home, they were going to spend several days with me, my mother staying on for a bit after my father went home. I thought their willingness to spend more time with me showed an effort on their part to strengthen our relationship. I hoped the time we spent together would enable us to know each other better and differently.

From my parents' viewpoint, my being in therapy confirmed their belief that I was nuts. I suspected they saw the meeting with Gail as an opportunity to tell her how nuts I was. My willingness to have a session with them showed how much I trusted Gail to believe and support me. Though I didn't see my parents' agreement to this session as resulting from a change in our relationship, I hoped it would

---

1 Passover meal during which the Haggadah is read.

produce information that would clarify the tension and conflict I sensed in my childhood.

I had no intention of telling my parents about my brother at this time. And I hadn't yet remembered that my grandmother had abused me. I wanted to enjoy their visit. I wanted them to enjoy my company. I was very logical in the way I approached the question of how and when to tell them that Ted had abused me. I thought I was still too unsure of myself to withstand a negative reaction from them. I was afraid if they disbelieved or blamed me, I would disbelieve and blame myself. I hoped that if our relationship improved before I dropped the bombshell, my parents might accept the truth. I ignored my internal pressure to dump the secret of my brother's abuse. I dismissed my anger over keeping it. And I underestimated my belief in myself.

*   *   *   *   *

MAY 2

I saw goslings in the Jewish Community Centre creek yesterday — seven puffballs paddling after the geese. I had such a pleasant day. I bought a brass floor lamp for the living room and two flowering plants. I read for awhile, then talked to Alma until 2:00 a.m. She said "Cold Where the Universe Ends" gave her goosebumps.

MAY 4

The apartment is lovely, if I do say so myself. I put up shelves in the bedroom and painted today.

MAY 7

I feel like I've stepped back a pace. I suppose to be the "new me" with my parents' visit looming is too hard right now. Yet I haven't totally returned to my old ways of being, though I feel vulnerable.

What would I be like without the weight of having to make up for Mum's and Dad's experiences in the war? It is beyond conception. There's always a shadow of death looming, the knowledge that all moments pass and then there are no more. Could I really live in the moment and savour it completely?

MAY 12

Yeoww!!!

Ann called this morning and asked if I was wired for sound. Yes, and sight and colour and movement.

D-day is here. I pick Mum up this afternoon.

It's 3:00. Mum will be here in six minutes! I just don't want to cry when I see her.

MAY 13

I've been up since 6:00 — diarrhea and nausea. Last night I showed Mum the bit I'd written about my feelings toward her and Mama when I was little. Mum was cool. She said I felt that way because I was nuts, not because our family was in any way like I described. She said Mama never interfered and that my feelings about the war came from my own head. I was difficult from the day I was born, different from Ted and Ellen. She gave me a lot of love and attention. I insisted that my perceptions were equally valid and real, but I don't think I got through to her. I asked her about the summer I turned five, and she said: (a) she didn't notice a change and (b) she thought I changed because I started school, or because she was away, or perhaps because I thought Mama was taking her place. She told me she realized that it was a mistake to stay in Israel as long as she did that summer because she missed Dad and Ted missed home. It hurts that she didn't say she missed me and wasn't concerned about how I might miss her. She looked shocked when I told her how Mama often said that she and Dad were frail and I had to take care of them.

I'm glad I showed Mum what I wrote, though her reaction angered and disappointed me. I'd hoped she would be compassionate and warm. My foiled expectations make me realize how far I have to go before I can tell them about Ted. Mum may always think I am, or was, nuts. It upholds the family picture. Otherwise the family was less than ideal. I don't always have to accept that role. I'll have to learn to relate to her without needing her to validate my perception. Is that possible?

My sick stomach comes from a turmoil of feelings, conflict between refusing and assuming my role in the family. I'm not ready to relinquish it, and not able to accept it.

Mum suggested I buy a trundle bed, expandable if a man stays over ("you're a healthy woman" — imagine her saying that!). She said I deserved better than Eugene, and I agreed. To that she said the Messiah must be coming.

MAY 14

Mum and Dad and I talked yesterday. I heard a lot of interesting things. Dad said they were still children in their mid-thirties. They consulted Mama about everything. Their big rebellion was buying Mum a coat without discussing it first with Mama. She told everyone that Mum would be lost without her, unable to raise her children. Mum told me that she should have had her head examined because Mama was a "half-wife." Dad said he used to alternate taking Mum and Mama to the movies. One week he took Mum, and the next week Mama.

When they first came to Canada and Ted was a baby, Dad suggested Mama might want her own life. She was offended. (I think she wanted theirs.) I asked why Mama didn't work. Mum told me that Mama took a job, but quit after a few days. So Mum had to work in a factory while Mama stayed home with Ted until Mum got pregnant with me. At which point Mama went out to work so she could earn the money for her first trip to Israel. When Mum was working, she and Dad washed the floors on the weekend because Mama said she worked so hard taking care of Ted. They never took any money from Mama. She travelled from time to time and they hoped she'd remarry. The first time Mama went to Israel, they didn't know how they'd manage without her advice. They felt like children whose parents have gone away. When she came back from that trip, she stayed at home with Mum until after we moved to the new house and Ellen was born. At that time I was just turning six. In the new house Mama and I shared a room but she was out working during the day.

Mum told me she started to become independent when I was nine, learning to drive at her friend's instigation (Mama hated her friend), joining a women's organization, and becoming more active. I remember at that time Mama stirring up trouble, saying to Ted "Don't you think Mum spends too much time on the telephone?" Mum told me she tried to cause grief between her and Dad using a similar line.

Even when Mum was forty, Mama criticized the way she cleaned the fridge. Mum said, "I'm forty years old. Don't you think I know how to clean out a fridge?"

Mama answered, "Doesn't a mother have the right to teach her child?"

Mum said she practically pushed Mama out the door. That's when Mama went looking for a husband, first on the cruise to Israel, then in Florida.

I asked them if they were aware that during the winter I was nine, whenever I came home from Hebrew school I peed on the porch just as I rang the doorbell. They said they didn't know.

Mum and Dad still believe that any expression of anger is wrong: Mum because Mama and Grandfather always fought and Dad because his father had a bad temper. When Dad was four, his father got some herring that was too dry and he threw the plate at the wall. Dad said his world shattered as the plate shattered.

I insisted that my perceptions were real and that my behaviour resulted from what was going on around me. I didn't get very far. I still want their validation. I must grow out of that.

Something that made me want to strangle them: Mum saying, "The most important thing about tomorrow (seeing Gail) is to be honest. Don't protect your daughter."

MAY 15

The session with Gail was much easier than I expected. She asked Mum and Dad basic questions about their own family history and ours. Little of what they said was news to me. I got a lot more information from them yesterday. Still, it was neat to see how they responded to Gail's questions. One thing that was interesting: Dad described me with Eugene as being under a spell. He said Eugene would spout the most utter nonsense and I'd look at him as if he were a god.

I'm stressed out, stretched thin, but I think things are going well. I'm not sure if Mum's listening, but I'm being myself and trying to be heard. She asked about what spurred me to separate from Eugene. I explained how it was not a case of a naive young thing being spellbound, but my total feeling of worthlessness and need to care for someone that kept me trapped. I left Eugene because therapy helped me discover my worth. She heard me enough to ask what had caused me to feel so worthless. I said there were a number of factors that were reinforced a million times by an experience I wasn't ready to talk about yet. I told her it was as if I'd been in a fire. Normal skin burns in a fire but you can graft healthy tissue onto the damaged skin and it slowly grows into healthy tissue. I emphasized that I was a normal person who had normal reactions to a destructive environment, now going through a healing process.

I'm really happy and excited about this visit but I have to pull back and realize this is just the beginning. I have to validate myself.

After Mum met Ann, she said Ann seems very levelheaded. I agreed and added she's got a lot of common sense. Mum said Ann was the opposite of me — I'm a dreamer.

MAY 16

Mum and I had a pleasant morning — breakfast together and window-shopping. Mum is revealing more of herself to me.

MAY 18

I can't believe I'm okay, all in one piece and pleased with myself. I told Mum about the abuse. It happened like this.

When Gail asked Mum why she thought I was a difficult child, she said I didn't clean up my room or help around the house voluntarily. It struck me that those are normal enough. It occurred to me later that Mum was embroiled in conflict with Mama, who was also causing trouble between Mum and Dad. I was difficult for her because she wasn't up to dealing with a child. At the same time Mama told her she was incapable of being a mother. Mum couldn't recognize her difficulties as stemming from her own upbringing and her situation with Mama, nor could she accept Mama's accusation. So she attributed her difficulties (and still does) to my being crazy, a problem child. The whole family also relied on my craziness to avoid facing the family problems.

Every few minutes as we discussed Mama and my childhood Mum would say that Ted and Ellen weren't affected, only I was. Therefore it was my problems that caused my reaction. I pointed out that Ted and Ellen may have been affected in ways that weren't apparent to her. I was irritated.

Saturday evening we had a lovely time. I felt relaxed and ate well for the first time all week. I invited several friends to have dinner with Mum and me. We talked about music, poetry, movies.

When I took Mum back to the hotel she invited me up. I felt alert and happy, so I went. We ended up discussing Mama again. Mum told me that she'd had it a thousand times worse than me. Mum and Dad nearly divorced when I was a baby because Mama kept telling her Dad was withdrawn and didn't talk about his feelings. When Dad decided to further his education, Mum supported him. Mama said to her, "You stupid. Don't you know he'll leave you?"

Out of the blue Mum told me that Mama and Grandfather were sexually incompatible. She was aware of that as a child, before the war. I said to Mum it was strange, I'd always had a double image of Mama as being asexual and very sexual. Mum said Mama was very sexual. I asked her what Mama did all those years before she remarried. Mum said that women masturbate, even married women do, and also, maybe ... her voice trailed off and I thought — maybe Mama abused Ted and/or me.

Well, thinking about Mama, hearing that I was the only one who was affected, listening to how Mum had it so rough just became too much. I wanted to tell her, had been thinking of the abuse all week. Every time I said Ted may have been affected in other ways, I thought "Don't tell, you haven't planned for it. Gail said you weren't ready. Call your friends. They'll tell you not to. Don't do this, it's the wrong time." Mum noticed my struggle and commented on it. I told her there was something I really wanted to tell her, but it wasn't the right time. She said "Don't tell me, then."

I answered (contrary as always): "Ted sexually abused me."

Mum: "I don't believe you. I simply don't believe you. How could you let it go on? How could you let it go on? Why didn't you tell me?"

She said I should have stopped it, I should have told her. It was my fault for not telling. She was a perfect mother in a perfect home that encouraged openness. She can't, for her own sake, see the secrecy, confusion, tension.

I felt terrible for telling her without Dad present, unplanned, before discussing it with Gail. I was devastated. I thought I shouldn't have told her. It was wrong. I didn't deserve to live.

I knew I wasn't helping things by punishing myself, but I couldn't help it.

I cried. Mum said "What's done is done. You've told me and now I have to deal with it."

She said she could go to sleep, so I called Cheryl and went over there. I cried and she hugged me. I was able to sleep for a couple of hours and felt a bit better when I woke up.

Sunday morning I went back to the hotel. Mum had told Dad. He called and said he felt very bad. Was there anything he could do for me now? I said he was by not turning away from me. He asked why they would. I answered, "Because I've told you something painful. Friends of mine have told their families and they turned away from them rather than deal with it."

Dad started to cry, saying "That's terrible. That's terrible." I cried too. He asked me how I felt (a first). I said I was scared because there was so much unknown.

Mum and I went for a walk and she told me:

— Ted was dating and having sex with his girlfriends during the time he was abusing me. (How does she know?)

— As a girl she saw her brother masturbate and it upset her.

— When she was eleven, the president of the synagogue made her sit on his lap while he masturbated. She stayed away from him after that.

— She was always worried about one of us kids being sexually abused *by someone within the family.*

— She was always looking for signs (she couldn't say what), but she never saw anything.

— She thought by teaching me "the facts of life" she was protecting me (no wonder she told me all about sex and contraception when I was five, though it was so far above me I don't remember it).

— Dad always said men have uncontrollable sexual urges, to which I replied that even so, Ted could have gone to a woman or girl his own age, or, Mum added, he could have masturbated.

— In the new house Mama refused to live in the basement apartment because that would have been below her dignity.

— Mum mothered Mama.

— She thinks one in two women are sexually abused as children, it's almost inevitable.

— She never discussed her concerns about sexual abuse with Dad.

— It made a big difference to her that intercourse did not take place.

After I took Mum to the airport, I called several friends and began to feel myself again. Mum said Dad would want to sweep it under the carpet, but they would have to confront Ted.

MAY 19

A letter, never sent:

Dear Mum and Dad:

I called this evening because I was concerned about how you were feeling. I wondered whether you had talked to Ted and how that affected your reaction to what I'd told you about the abuse.

You said that it was a matter of perspective, there was no child molesting and no abuse. Ted has suffered enough. The family name must not be besmirched.

I resent your concern over besmirching the family name. It's already besmirched. Ted did sexually abuse me. I was a child and he was an adult. He was responsible for what happened, and is responsible for the consequences.

I am angry because you are not listening to me. I would like you to get to know me better, but you can't if you want me to pretend that the abuse is in the past and forgotten. The aura of secrecy over your reaction to what I and Ted told you accomplishes nothing. It perpetuates the fog that obscures your vision of me and mine of you.

I'm sad because I feel shut out. I wasn't able to express my concern for you. I'm not able to share with you the effects the abuse has had on me. I agree that we shouldn't dwell in the past, but I am an incest survivor. That is an important part of me and always will be. It isn't over and done with simply by my telling you that I was abused and your letting Ted know that you're aware of it. To deal with it, in my view, we need to understand clearly how each of us perceives what happened and how we're affected by it. We need to get rid of family secrets.

You said I must become well. I was never sick. The incest experience was terrible for me. I felt pain, violation, confusion, anger, betrayal. I felt completely alone, and could survive only by numbing myself. I am no longer numb. I am now dealing with the feelings I couldn't deal with as a child. Those feelings were normal reactions to sexual abuse. I developed normal defense mechanisms to allow me to survive. I no longer need those mechanisms and am growing into myself as I leave them behind.

I love you very much and I hope that sometime I'll be able to tell you what I've written today.

MAY 20

I'm shaky and a bit nauseous. I reread "Cold Where the Universe Ends." I felt stronger afterward. It reminded me of who I am, where I've been and where I'm going.

I think it was right for me to tell Mum and Dad and this was the right time for me. I wanted them to know. Nevertheless, it's hard for me to realize how much pain I've caused them. It's hard for me not to feel responsible for their hurt. But I couldn't have gone on being myself and hiding the abuse. It's too large a part of my experience. I'd got too fed up with hearing how I was the only one affected by my environment. Not that this changes Mum and Dad's view. They still believe that Ted is wonderful and lives a wonderful life, that my life was a mess, that I was the one with all the problems. But at least

I've said what I had to say. My words are no longer lost, choked off in my throat.

I just wish I didn't feel so awful. It hurts terribly that Mum and Dad have shut me out. I'm afraid I've lost a family except for "How are you and how's the weather?"

IX

The Face of Anger

As the originator of the family secrets, my grandmother was at the centre of a web in which each of us was caught. We were tied to her by strings of deception which protected her abusiveness from discovery and confrontation. Our movements were confined by this web, restricting every aspect of our lives.

Attached to my grandmother, my parents weren't free to grow up. They remained needy children with limited ability to nurture us kids so that we could grow up. We got big, still caught in the family web, unable to be ourselves or live free, grown-up lives. A new generation of secrets was created by my brother. I imagine him at the centre of a web of his own, spun off from my grandmother, perpetuated by deception.

To free ourselves from the web, we needed to let go the lies, myths and dishonest behaviour. After my grandmother remarried, my parents began slowly to distance themselves from her suffocating presence although they kept in close touch with her and she spent several months a year with us. In time, my parents made a life that was their own. They developed relationships that fit their values, rather than my grandmother's, rejecting many of her bitter lies to do so. They reached for their dreams and found them.

The measure of my parents' independence showed in their ability to see my therapist, to give me helpful information about my childhood and to meet me part way in rebuilding our connection. Yet they continued to conceal my grandmother's abusive nature. They were not able to face the evil she engendered through physically and sexually abusing me, nor the evil still hidden — the rest of my family's secrets. My parents pulled back from me as soon as I exposed a part of that evil by disclosing my brother's abuse. They responded to the

84

truth with denial, coldness, and rejection, just as they did when I was a child.

Despite believing me, my sister also turned away. After I told my parents about the abuse, Ellen spoke to me once. It took a while but I finally got the hint when her husband told me she couldn't come to the phone because her hands were in a chicken. Twice a year she left good wishes on my answering machine: Rosh Hashana (New Year) and my birthday.

My brother's only concern was to retain as much of the family deception as possible despite my exposing his secret. He showed no interest in the truth — that would require him to acknowledge his responsibility for abusing me.

My fears of family relationships consisting of "How are you and the weather?" were realized for several years. Once I rejected deception it seemed that nothing else was left. No one in my family could accept or relate to the person I really was. They needed to view their lives through the veil of myths, despite the cost to them in feeling, being, and doing. I could not have the family I wanted.

I expected this situation to continue, unchanged. But, over time, the shake up had positive repercussions as well as negative. Ellen started talking to me again. My parents and I came to terms. The love between us endured and, though there are limitations and painfully rough patches, we have found ways to genuinely relate. I grew, and so did they.

Despite their limitations, my parents gave me what they were unable to give themselves. My father, the most brilliant person I know, thought he was stupid until well into his middle age. He still doesn't recognize his vision and sensitivity, which I value so greatly. He believes that he doesn't communicate well on a personal level and nothing I say convinces him that he can communicate clearly, deeply, and lovingly. Yet in the midst of suffering from lack of self-worth, he valued me, sowing the kernel of self-esteem that enabled me to grow, even in my marriage, to rid myself of Eugene and get the help I needed.

Though my mother was unable to face the abuse in her family life to gain her own freedom, she gave me the strength to deal with the abuse in my life so I could be free. I looked up to her as a model of courage, confronting pain square in the face as she went to schools to talk about her experiences in the Holocaust. She found a way to nurture something positive out of devastation, transcending the horror by giving meaning to what she did with it. She became a woman capable of lifelong growth, inspiring me to transcend the horror in my life, to grow into myself and give back to the world with my own special gifts.

"Cold Where the Universe Ends" was the first fruit of that inspiration. Writing it revealed myself to me. Sharing it with friends revealed me to them. Their response — affection, compassion, belief and respect — gave me an inkling of real intimacy, the warm glow of being cherished as me, secure because I could never fail at being myself. This was in direct contrast to the false intimacy I'd experienced at home, a closeness that was based on playing roles, awarded and withdrawn to support the family deception. The positive reaction I got from sharing my reality reinforced the pride and strength I gained from writing it, enabling me to stand up to my parents, telling them the truth so I could go on.

Once I accepted and told the truth, my next step was to deal with it. Dealing with it meant feeling and expressing what I'd been unable to feel and express when I was abused. It meant replacing misinformation with accurate information: from Gail, from group, from other people in my life I found trustworthy, from books. It meant getting to know myself, my likes and dislikes, strengths and weaknesses, experimenting with and practising new ways of being that suited me, my lifestyle and my relationships. It meant giving up my false outer self, slowly letting people know and respond to the real me.

I have experienced accepting the truth and dealing with it as a process that occurs over and over on deeper levels. In recovering from abuse, I had to accept the truth of all the different kinds of injury I suffered from each of my abusers. At every level I had to struggle with the real dangers and with the deception that kept me silent as a child. This struggle was often frustrating, always difficult. But each time I was able to find my voice, I reclaimed a greater portion of myself and a greater enjoyment of living.

*   *   *   *   *

MAY 22

I'm afraid that my anger will come flying out of control and then Gail will abandon me.

MAY 23

I feel rotten. I hit the couch with the tennis racket, felt an immediate relief, but then greater anxiety. I'm brimming over with painful feelings, shaky with them rocking against the wall of my control. Dear God, I'm so scared. I want to scream and cry and hide away, but I've got work to do.

MAY 24

Ted called. He said, "Well, I guess the secret's out." He asked what he could do to help within certain limits and conditions. I told him he could explain why. He said he doesn't remember. He doesn't know. In the midst of a long, meaningless statement about terms and conditions, he said he wouldn't take my interrogating him. I told him he sounded cold-blooded, like he was talking about affairs of state, but he sexually abused me. I yelled a bit, saying I was sick and angry over what he did to me. I was a child and he was responsible. He said he wouldn't take the blame for all my problems. I told him I wasn't blaming him for my problems, I was angry with him for abusing me.

He said what difference did it make why. I asked him, "If I punched your kid in the head wouldn't you want an explanation?"

He answered that if twenty years ago I tripped and fell over his kid he wouldn't expect me to remember why. I got angry and said he was responsible for abusing me. He said he wouldn't take the blame. I told him he fucked me around. He said something about my becoming "cured." I said I was curing myself by expressing my feelings and not developing an ulcer.

I asked Ted if he'd see Gail with me. He said he'd be willing to see Gail under certain conditions, which he didn't specify, except that he wants her to call him at home. I said I appreciated his calling. I still think he's an asshole. I have a feeling he's under family pressure. His big line is "what can I do to help in 1987?"

After I spoke to him, I hit the couch with the tennis racket. It helped. On thinking it over, I'm not ready to have a therapy session with him.

MAY 26

I wrote another fake letter to Ted after hitting the couch with a tennis racket. When will this end? Gail talked about how much energy it takes to keep my anger contained. Yes, and it makes me feel tight inside and miserable. But then releasing it, I feel drained and sad. I wonder what my life would be like if I had that energy to live with, to write or dance or laugh.

One good thing about my anger is that it's cleaning the couch.

MAY 30

Mum now denies what she told me when we went for a walk that Sunday. She presents one face to me and a different one to Ellen. The trouble occurs when the two meet, as by my telling Ellen that Mum had been molested as a child. Mum then denies and retreats to the "nicer" face. All my life Mum has been changing what she says. Yet it still stuns me and makes me question myself. But not as much and not as long as it used to.

JUNE 5

Reading *Cry Hard And Swim*,[1] a first-person incest account, I have tears in my eyes, tears of happiness and gratitude because the book speaks to me so much. It makes me want to give back some of the satisfaction I received, to contribute my words to the song.

There is a great song of life, a song of joy and pain, laughter, tears, silliness, despair, triumph. The sky is part of it, and rocks, trees, animals. Each person is a part of it, with his and her own special beauty, with everything she and he create, with everything we do, small or great. Gail is part of it and the work she does. The receptionist

---

1   Jacqueline Spring, *Cry Hard and Swim* (London: Virago Press, 1987).

at the agency is part of it. I'm part of it by virtue of being human, but I want my part of the song to be as full and melodic as possible.

I had such fun at the art gallery today. I'm happy and tired. Life is so beautiful, how can I contain it?

JUNE 6

Gail is going on holiday in six weeks. Well, here we go again.

JUNE 7

Thinking about Gail's holiday, I remembered the dream I had last fall about the therapist who, trying to get me to remember childhood sex play with a girlfriend, instead lost me to a memory of Mama.

JUNE 8

I felt awful all weekend. I slept and slept. When I was awake my head hurt and I had no energy. I feel sad and angry. It's hard because I don't know what happened. Why was it that bad to be left with Mama?

JUNE 9

I feel terrible, although there's a little part of me that is relieved.

Last night I remembered Mama's hands over mine, holding them to her breasts when I was four or five.

JUNE 10

As I was lying down, one of my drawings came to my mind. It became a picture of giant legs and a vagina and my baby fist in it.

JUNE 12

It smells wonderful after the rain. I don't feel very real this morning: an escape, I suppose.

Ann gave me a lesson in doing laundry yesterday. I always thought my laundry was grey because of the machine, but guess what? It's because I mixed colours! I'm impressed and foresworn to do laundry Ann's way.

JUNE 13

I couldn't wait to see Gail today and dreaded it, thinking I couldn't tell her what I pictured. I'm anxious, my nerves raw, but I don't feel so impossible about telling her.

JUNE 14

I napped on and off all day. In the last sleep I had, I realized that Mama did abuse me and it is a good thing I'm writing about it. I woke up feeling elated. The elation has faded, but I'm holding onto to the rightness I felt, though doubt niggles at me again.

JUNE 15

I bought the prettiest pink and crimson carnations this morning.

Talking to Dad yesterday, I asked him year by year when Mama was home and when she was working. The dates he gave me fit what I've remembered.

JUNE 17

I feel like I did in early spring, as if something is changing, growing, unfolding inside me. I feel like a rocket. Stage one has dropped away and stage two is preparing to drop. And then I'll soar up into the far reaches of my imagination.

JUNE 18

I had a nightmare, screaming because I didn't want to see someone's face. It's a recurring theme in my nightmares — a face slowly appearing or suddenly changing into something I'm terrified to see. When I woke up I tried to think of a peaceful image, but I couldn't gather my thoughts together. I remembered, though, how Gail has said that my dreams are part of a process: from nightmare to changes in my life. I felt less scared then.

JUNE 22

I read Cheryl "Scrambled Eggs," a story I wrote about Mama. She said I should change it. Talking to Ann afterward, I started defending my memories and the awfulness of the family situation.

Ann said I didn't have to explain it to her, she accepted it. She told me to forget Cheryl, get myself a nice lunch and have a nap.

JUNE 25

My head hurts so badly. I wish I could cry.

JUNE 29

I'm angry with Dad, and sad. He didn't protect me from Mama, and he could have. He should have. It hurts that although he loved me and I loved him, he abandoned me. He shielded himself at my expense.

JULY 4

With telling Gail I am angry at her for going on vacation and crying a bit every other day, I find myself feeling more peaceful. Yesterday I dreamt that if I remember anything, I will be able to bear it. Then I had a sweet sleep.

JULY 6

I'm sitting on the window ledge, crying. I feel like I have a hole in my heart, a terrible hurt deep inside me. Why didn't Mum take care of me? Mama hurt me without reason. She abused me and Mum didn't protect me. Mum sacrificed me. I was so scared and hurt and sad, so powerless and alone.

I can bear it but God it's painful. I'm going to count my blessings, now:
— each time I cry, the ice inside me melts a little more.
— the plants are growing like mad.
— I've put the blinds up in the bedroom and they look fine.
— I'm going to Ann's to swim and sew on Wednesday.
— the yellow flowers Mary brought me are lovely.
— I've got plenty of business lined up.
— I'm going to be okay, and someday I'll be free.

JULY 11

It is hot! I've been writing "The Face of Anger." Version one started when I realized who the face of anger belonged to. I wrote version two when I remembered one of the incidents that sparked my vision of that face. Version three begins after two weeks of remembering and crying.

JULY 11

THE FACE OF ANGER — Three

As long as I can remember, writing has been a way for me to express my view of the world, reflecting my true feelings however much I doubted and denied my perceptions to myself. In all my poems and stories though, there is nothing about my grandmother. Everything connected with her was part of a deep, forgotten hurt so terrible that even the part of me that writes, which has always preserved some sense of who I really am, couldn't approach the breathless pain of my secret.

My secret was contained in an image I had: looking at the back of a head as it slowly turned, knowing that my world would be destroyed if I saw the face. As long as I didn't see it, my secret could remain forgotten. The slowly appearing face of power, face of evil, face of anger, of something familiar turned monstrous, haunted my nightmares. All through the years, I was able to wake up before I saw it. My sleeping self knew the secret, speaking to me night after night, but I couldn't listen. To listen would mean to feel that terrible hurt, and that I couldn't do. All I could do was survive and forget until I was grown up enough to protect the child I was while I uncovered the secret.

When I began to remember, I'd lie in bed and hold myself close while I hurt. My secret lived in a cold pit and I was falling forever, each memory a fresh and deeper pain. After a while I found that I could hurt sitting up, and that I didn't hurt all the time. Then I discovered that I, the woman of iron who didn't cry, didn't ache, the doer and mover, could cry and not fall apart. At first I choked back my tears after a few seconds, feeling silly and strange. But as I began to cry more easily, it was as if a little bit of my pain was let go, and the heavy burden of so many years of containing my secret eased, until finally I could cry with all the ache and bewilderment of the little girl I'd been.

In my returning memory I saw myself beside the kitchen table, too little to see over the top. I was lonely and sad. My grandmother was standing across from me at the counter. I asked her for a glass of water. She whirled around, her anger so fierce that I watched in horror as the back of her head turned to show her face. My heart jumped. She'd looked so calm with her back toward me. How could I have made such a terrible mistake? Now the world was crashing around me. She was a monster. She hit me. My head hit the floor with a loud crack, too loud, because she was picking me up and shaking me until my teeth chattered, her face close to mine, jaw clenched, ugly and hateful. I felt as if I were broken in little jagged pieces jarring against each other as she shook me, cutting me inside and out till I couldn't feel anything any more. When she put me down I was still wobbly, as if I would never stop shaking inside, all the little broken pieces mixed up and tumbling around inside me. She smiled through the ugliness and taking my hand in hers, took me into her bedroom.

My grandmother's explosions of anger were usually followed by sexual abuse. I thought it was part of the punishment. I was being punished because I felt too much, too sad or angry or happy; or for being alive and being me, because I was supposed to be my grandmother's hand and had no right to be my own self; or for no reason at all. My grandmother just turned my world topsy-turvy whenever she pleased.

I felt crazy and disjointed in the everyday world where I wasn't being abused. If I cried, I was being silly, unreasonable, stubborn — I knew I had no right to feel hurt unless I could prove that something was wrong, and I couldn't prove anything. Everyone else seemed to believe in the mask of love my grandmother wore. How could I describe the way it cracked and revealed the face of anger out of control? No one would believe me. I hardly believed myself. It was too awful.

I felt inconsequential, like a voiceless rag, used and discarded at my grandmother's whim. It hurt that she hated me so much, even more that it wasn't personal. It was as if I was in the hands of a god whose actions were beyond my understanding. This god lived high on a cloud above me, beyond my feeble shouts and prayers, but reached down with a mighty fist to tear from me its due. I felt as if there was a pit inside me, a profound despair I couldn't bear. Inside that pit was the loneliness, sadness and pain of being so little and so badly hurt by my grandmother, someone who should have loved and cared for me. I knew that if I fell into the pit, I'd fall forever and be lost. Instead I forgot what my grandmother did to me.

My sleeping self still remembered so that for twenty-five years I watched the face of anger slowly turning, and screamed. It remembered so that when I was strong enough to look into the pit, the memories of my secret were waiting for me and I could reclaim the little girl I was, with all her sadness and hurt, as myself.

JULY 14

An amazing thing. While I was telling Gail how angry I was with Mama, I felt as if a vise clamped around my chest. Gail had me talk to the vise. I felt silly when I spoke as me, but powerful when I spoke for the vise. Gradually it switched. I got angry with the vise part of myself for intimidating me. I realized it could make me afraid. It could stop me from expressing my feelings. But it couldn't stop me from feeling. It couldn't control my imagination. It couldn't stop all my avenues of expression and if I was afraid, it wouldn't last forever. It had no power over me. It was wonderful, amazing! And I did it myself. My anger gave rise to strength. There was power in my voice!

JULY 17

I'm angry with Gail because she's going away, leaving me with my feelings. She says I'm giving birth to my adult self.

LABOUR

Just like childbirth,
it's adult birth, you said.
I'd like to see you in labour
for over a year, no end in sight.
Hey, where's the anesthetic,

put me out and wake me when it's over.
It's easy for you to talk
with professional compassion and distance,
"see you next time," shut the door,
and all the mess walks out with me,
leaving your office pure and clean.

God said, "I will greatly multiply
thy pain and thy travail; in pain
thou shalt bring forth."
God meant it, too —
that's what I get for knowing good
and evil.
It doesn't matter that I was just a kid
when the serpent throttled my childhood.
I still got kicked out of Eden,
I still have to squeeze my life between pains,
bringing forth.
Bringing up is more like it —
a shit load of stinking vomit.

Hey God,
why don't you put your finger
on the serpents for a change,
let them twist in helpless fear.

And you out there
in your antiseptic room,
take your plastic words
and shove them.
Fuck off.

JULY 18

For me, Gail's holiday is the *end*. I don't have much faith in the
beginning. To trust and believe in beginnings is frightening. Time

stands still for me at the point where Gail goes on holiday, as if there's a wall there. Once the day comes, time starts to move again.

JULY 22

I just read the letter I wrote to myself when I was fifteen to be "read when in need of a little encouragement." I bawled my eyes out. It was as if the me at fifteen was reaching a hand across the years to me, the adult, and to the little girl in me who wasn't encouraged or nurtured: "I don't know why I was put here, nor why anyone else was and will probably never know. But once I am here, let me use this gift of life and all my talents to DO SOMETHING. God willing that when it's time for me to die, I will have done something to help this world and its creatures. God give me strength and wisdom."

That desire to live life to the fullest and to Do Something was lost in me for so many years. In the last few months I've become aware of it again: to create something that brings hope or beauty to other people's lives, making my part of the song of life as full and clear as I can, using all my gifts, being myself, giving of myself, and receiving from other people in an exchange of love, humour, tenderness, beauty and respect that flows out into the world and makes it a better place.

JULY 23

My wandering Jew has bloomed! Beautiful little crimson flowers on the side facing the window. I feel as though it's a manifestation of what's happening inside me.

JULY 24

I had my last session with Gail for a couple of weeks. Time can start to move again.

$\overline{x}$

My Blood

A newborn infant is totally dependent on adults. As the infant grows, gradually discovering itself and the world, it becomes less dependent, though still needing the care of adults in its life. Children whose needs are met mature and leave home to make their own lives. We who were abused did not get the safety, guidance and affirmation we needed to grow up and leave. We have jobs, families of our own, responsibilities. Yet we live in both the present and the past. We are the adult getting by and we are the child reliving an abusive past, trying to satisfy unmet needs behind the scenes of our adult life. Controlled by the actions and reactions of this unhappy child, we cannot give full attention to our adult lives.

To give the child in us what our family did not, we allow ourselves to depend on a caring, reliable adult who can guide us in our self-discovery. This reliable adult, say a therapist, satisfies personal needs through other relationships. Because this person does not need us to satisfy her or him, we are free to grow in our own time and way, as is our right. By demonstrating care and reliability in words and actions, this person slowly earns our trust, creating a place of safety for us to explore our reality. This person is there to be depended on, to encourage our independence and to let us go when we're ready.

My dictionary says to depend means "to rely for support, maintenance, help," as in "children depend on their parents." I was not able to depend on my parents for help when I was abused, nor for support in expressing myself. They excused themselves through the myth that I was born independent and wilful, as if I were made of iron. I liked the myth. It made me feel powerful, instead of humiliated and abandoned. I was never a child. I was a woman of iron. Invulnerable. Abandonment and betrayal were nothing to me.

It was hard to let myself depend on Gail because it exposed my vulnerability. It was risky. What if she betrayed me the way my parents had? What if she abandoned me? Though it never happened, each time I stood in the reception area before my appointment, I waited for someone to tell me that Gail had left. It took a year and a half for me to trust that she would be there. Time eased my fears as I saw that Gail was different from my family. She was dependable. I could count on her to support, maintain and help me — during my sessions and by telephone if necessary. That was enough. But I didn't want less. And during Gail's holiday, I had to accept less. I had no choice. Despite what I wanted, she was going away for a time.

In the safety of my relationship to Gail, I gradually learned to acknowledge and express my wants. At first I felt ashamed of desires I thought were unreasonable, like not wanting Gail to go on vacation. But with Gail's encouragement, I began to express the feelings aroused in me by her holiday. Being left made me feel like the child I'd been — helpless, abandoned. Angry. Hurt. I had to be more self-reliant than I wanted to be, just like when I was little. As a child I wasn't capable of taking care of myself the way I had to. As an adult with adult resources, I could handle it when Gail was away. I just didn't want to.

To be independent is to be unconstrained and free from subjection, not depending upon something else for existence, says the dictionary. Real independence changes the family order when children grow up to lead their own lives. This was unacceptable in my family. Our existence depended on what the family needed from us to guard its secrets and maintain the status quo. Constrained by our assigned roles, none of us was permitted to be who we really were. In my family I was called independent because I didn't lean on anyone. I didn't belong. I was utterly lonely. My family's definition of independence was actually isolation. I didn't know that being independent meant leading my own life. I thought it meant keeping to myself in my silent cocoon.

A year and a half of therapy didn't make me my own person. But I was on my way. Little by little I was emerging from my cocoon, discovering to my surprise that I wasn't alone — though I couldn't yet trust or quite believe that. I still had a weakness for needy people but, as I learned to set limits, I found out who my real friends were. The ones who genuinely cared for me adjusted to the way I was changing. Others dropped away. Though losing friends hurt, I was also relieved, gaining time and energy for people who gave something back to me. Finding happiness and definition in my true self, I was ever so slowly becoming independent.

I gained confidence in what I was doing as my life got better and better. I believed in my right to depend on Gail. I believed in my right to become my own person as my dependence enabled me to grow up. This confidence was new and fragile. Sometimes the unfamiliarity felt scary and wrong. It was easy for me to be afraid that Gail would kick me out of therapy or in some other way abandon me. When she went on holiday the fact of my being left, even temporarily, inflamed my fears. It shook the foundation of my confidence. In that shaky state, the new information I absorbed during therapy got mixed up with old information I hadn't yet discarded. So as Gail encouraged my independence while she was away, I thought she was calling for my isolation. The recollection of that excruciating loneliness triggered an eruption of feelings and memories that began when Gail gave me the dates of her holiday and lasted till the day she left.

Being left reminded me in particular of the summer my mother went away, committing me to the care of my grandmother — a brutal, lonely time. The first year I was in therapy, Gail's holidays aroused feelings I associated with that summer, but none of the memories. To remember, I needed the support I didn't have as a child: my own adult strength, the dependability of my therapist, the belief and backing of my friends. That support became evident when I told my parents about my brother's abuse, spoke to him and dealt with my family's negative reaction. Being able to hold onto my own reality despite their denial showed me my strength. The help I got from Gail and my friends during that period demonstrated their reliability. I certainly didn't sit down and decide it was time to remember, but my internal regulator must have recognized that I could handle what I'd forgotten. I wasn't so sure myself. I was afraid of what those memories would reveal. I was afraid I couldn't bear it. The rational, adult part of me was considering what my parents had told me about my early childhood, fitting their information into my own impressions. This clearer picture of my childhood helped me understand how it had affected me, but there were missing pieces in my forgotten memories. These pieces unconsciously controlled my life through the reactions of the unhappy child in me. To see and heal the hurts of that child, I had to reclaim those memories. Gail's holiday was the catalyst that threw me over the hump of fear into the memories I needed to get on with my life.

*   *   *   *   *

AUGUST 27

The last couple of days have been awful. I hurt so much I keep thinking I can't stand it. I've hit the couch with the tennis racket, cried, written. Each time brought some ease for the moment but then the pain hit me again.

The good thing is that I didn't have to go through the strain of my usual remembering process: the nightmare, the feelings, the drawing, so scared of what's to come, and finally the relief of memory after a period of days, or even weeks. This memory came all at once: Mama's legs around me and my head against her vagina — the smell, the wetness. I feel like a ton of bricks fell on my head.

AUGUST 28

It was hard to tell Gail what I remembered. It was awful. And yet although I'm still shaky and headachy and weepy, I want to laugh. I'm so relieved. I showed anger during my session and nothing bad happened! I'm still here. Gail is still here. Remember Gail's hands strong on my back, telling me to breathe, to go on.

She said I have to keep trying to release anger as much as I can in as many ways as I can, even though the relief may only be momentary, because I'm sitting on a volcano and need to ease the pressure.

She suggested I do something nice for myself and I did. I bought cushions for the couch and a set of flatware with red handles. Both are things I've wanted for a while. I can enjoy them every day and say to myself "See — that's your reward for expressing your anger."

AUGUST 29
Whenever I woke up last night, I was terrified, gripped by an anxiety attack. Maybe as I get used to feeling and releasing this anger, it'll get easier. I made a granny doll out of scraps of denim, stuffed with carpet remnants. It makes a nice resounding thwack against the floor. It felt good to put some of my angry energy into making something. Just think what I'll be able to do with that energy when I'm done using it on my anger! That's my comfort in all this mess.

AUGUST 30
I can't imagine ever telling Mum and Dad about Mama abusing me.

SEPTEMBER 8
It's so nice to sit at home in my rocking chair, snug and smug (isn't life wonderful!).

I wrote to Ellen today, telling her how angry and hurt I feel about her never returning my calls. It's a family myth that we stand by each other in a crisis. It hides our distance. I'm willing to meet her more than halfway, but she's got to work at the relationship too.

SEPTEMBER 11
Laying on the grass, looking up at the trees. The leaves are starting to turn. Fall is so beautiful and exciting. It's the beginning of things, the new liturgical year and the school year. I've survived the heat of summer, hay fever and memories.

SEPTEMBER 20
I've framed my awards and actually hung them in public view where my clients can see them.

SEPTEMBER 22

Scraped my fist again hitting a cushion in Gail's office. I want to cry and yet I feel good with the satisfaction of saying something nasty when you really want to. The little girl inside me is clapping her hands and kicking up her heels, going, "Goody!" My anger feels stronger because more has come to the surface, but it is choking me less. And bouncing around inside me is a bubble of happiness. It contains the image of me as a little girl on a swing flying higher into the great blue sky.

SEPTEMBER 25

Every time I try to think about my session today my mind leaps away. It isn't because I was working on anger, or because I cried, though that was hard. It's because Gail supported me with her hands on my back. Being touched in a gentle way is overwhelming in the context of my life.

It reminds me by contrast of all the times I was vulnerable to someone who seemed powerful, and was touched in a horrible way. Something I like, something good, was made repugnant. It's as if someone who loves chocolate cake was forced to eat cakes filled with castor oil and Ex-lax, all the while craving real chocolate cake; and every so often being given a sliver of chocolate, just to whet her taste for it.

I think it was Mum who kept alive my belief that touch could be good. The way she stroked my hair, the way I cuddled against her in bed after Dad left for work, felt loving and safe.

SEPTEMBER 30

Hurray, it's nearly October, the golden month. This is such a ripe, contemplative time. Thinking about the year that's past, I wonder with excitement what the coming year holds.

I had the strangest sleep last night, dreaming and dreaming. In one of the dreams I was both a student and adult. Gail was a teacher, giving me some kind of test. I pictured a door and knew that something to do with Mama was behind it.

OCTOBER 1

MOTHER TO DAUGHTER

I loved to hear stories,
how it was
the lives
of my mothers,
back to the beginning
back to dancing
on the other side of the red sea,
passion, love, pain —
blood,
life that was, life that will be,
striving for joy,
survivors.
Lies.
Stories of the past
bright with Mama's courage
corroded
mirror cracks
Mama
a coward
a mean shrivelled soul
feeding on my body.
The mothers dance alone.
I am lost
cut off.

OCTOBER 2

MY BLOOD

In the mirror I see a portrait of my past: my mother's cheeks, my
grandmother's nose, my father's jaw, and all the others I never knew
who left a piece of themselves in me, the ones who died in the war.
When I look into my eyes, I see a photograph of my father's sisters
sitting on a park bench winding wool, their eyes so much like mine:

the one who could have been an artist, the one who gave my father her fountain pen for his bar mitzvah. There's so little for me to know, just scraps of my father's memories. My mother says she remembers nothing before the war. So there we are, my face made up of scraps and missing pieces.

I'm terrified that Mama will jump out of the mirror, shattering the pieces of me, and that I will be like her when she was abusing me: bitter, angry, powerful, hurting little helpless things. Mama is my blood too. It hurts me to think of that. It hurts because the nameless monster who abused me was my own grandmother. I was betrayed by my own flesh and blood. It hurts because to perceive her within myself is to acknowledge similarities between me and that monster. I can almost see the shards of glass flying from the mirror, and what will I find then — my grandmother, or who I really am?

The grown up me is quite rational about the whole thing: the idea of therapy is self-discovery, isn't it? And part of who I am is how I've come to be, from my mother on back; including my grandmother, especially including her because she is such an important person in my life and in my family. That's fine and dandy, but the little girl in me sure as hell doesn't trust adults or adult rationale. She's pounding her feet, screaming "Stop, I want to get off, here." Okay, how about if we take a peek and if it's too awful for words, we'll run for cover.

Like Mama, I know how to pick on someone's weak spot, while seeming to be untouchable myself. I can show my displeasure force-fully without saying a word. I can be mean. I can be bossy. I can be manipulative. I can be resentfully kind. I can pretend to be what I am not. I can refuse responsibility for my words.

Like Mama I am perceptive, strong-minded, and passionate. I am like her in my zest for life, my sense of humour, my love of colours, my pleasure in a place of my own, my taste for pretty smells and flowers, my enjoyment of living things.

This woman who fed a squirrel that came into the kitchen from the backyard could hurt and sexually abuse me. And if she could, and I am like her in some ways, could I? That's the thought that chills.

Mama fed that squirrel, but she was shocked when it got scared because the door blew closed, scratching her in its panic to get out.

She never fed it again. Mama liked living things as long as they were sweet and antiseptic. Everything around her had a right to exist only as it pleasured her. Otherwise she resented and hated it. I think that's why she was so bitter and angry when my parents tried to live a life of their own.

I respect living things because they have a right to be. I love my plants and my cats because they're alive and beautiful with their own specialness. I cherish them.

Mama had no regard for anything on this earth except herself. She could abuse me because I was just an object for her use, no more than a pillow to punch if she was angry, or a vibrator to use if she needed sexual release. I know that we all have the right to exist as best we can. No one has the rights of ownership over another living thing. I know the difference between a pillow, a vibrator, and a person.

I am like my grandmother in some ways but I'm not her. That's something I need to turn over in my mind so that I can say it to myself in my weak and fearful moments.

I want to look in the mirror and see myself, the past within me, my past, my family past, my historical past, and beyond that my own specialness that's just me. I've clouded the mirror with myths that filled in the scraps and missing pieces: historical myths of brave and true foremothers; family myths of secrets and superiority; personal myths of superhuman strengths and demonic flaws. What I took to be a shattering of my image just seems that way because I'm wiping the mirror one section at a time. It leaves a patchy reflection, part memory, part myth, part truth. As I start to see Mama in me, I'm picking up the rag again to wipe the mirror. My hand's shaky. I'm scared. But I believe that I'll see someone worth knowing. This is just the beginning.

OCTOBER 7

As I was falling asleep this afternoon, I realized that Mama tried to squish the life out of me, just like Eugene. That's what I felt when she locked me in the closet until the fight went out of me. To remember that made me feel sad until I imagined rocking in a chair, cuddling that three-year-old inside me. I fell asleep — a good, restful sleep.

OCTOBER 13

I feel as if I've lived my life in the broom closet that Mama locked me into when she was mad. Shutting out betrayal, shutting out comfort, I've stayed there, holding the door closed with that iron will of mine.

I'd rush into danger, risk anything to be needed, take on as much responsibility as was tossed in my lap, tell you anything you want to know about me without fear. That substituted for closeness. I gave the impression of transparency, but I didn't reveal my feelings. They were still back in the closet, hidden, quiet. Accept anything from someone else? Impossible. I'd never let them into the closet where the part of me that was needy cringed. People saw the mask I made up when I was five, someone who always seemed to have things together, civilized, serene. In reality I was someone whose knuckles were white, gripping control so tightly.

OCTOBER 16

I am angry at Mama's abuse making me choke off the sexual part of me. I'm angry at having to work so hard to voice myself, whether crying or shouting or releasing sexual pleasure.

OCTOBER 18

I went to the nursery today and got some light soil mix. I repotted several plants. I love doing things like that. I feel peaceful, alive with the smell of wet earth.

OCTOBER 22

My wandering Jew bloomed again! Hurray!

OCTOBER 23

I've been so frustrated over this crying business. I feel stuck because I can't let myself cry again in front of Gail, no matter how choked up I feel. I have to keep control, always control.

OCTOBER 24

Good morning! I slept well and long last night, woke up feeling renewed. I had a good dream: there was a peace delegation of women from Russia. It was supposed to be just a gesture, without meaning anything, but a bunch of us decided to make it meaningful by getting to know the women and having them get to know us. I became very good friends with one Russian woman. We were walking in the park and we started to fly. Other people around us were also flying. We came to rest on the grass. One man who was a bird and a person stood up to touch each person, making everyone a bird and a person too. People were reaching out to him to be touched. He would not touch them unless they reached out to show they were willing. I was afraid, thinking maybe it wasn't true, they just wanted to believe it, and the touch would be bad. Then one of the men who'd been touched stood up to touch other people. At first I thought he was touching them with a withered hand, but then I saw it was a wing, glimmering blue and green. The wing shimmered away, and I saw his hand. So I knew it was true. I reached out to be touched, and I became a bird and a person. So did my friend. Being a bird and a person meant we'd always be able to fly, be free, and call to one another. When we were all standing I got separated from my friend. I was really upset because she'd leave for Russia and I'd never see her again. I told one of the bird people. She chirped and another one chirped and another, and so the message was passed on. They found her and the crowd opened. We ran to each other and hugged. I told her how I'd been so upset and how glad I was to see her. The dream ended with us hugging and laughing and crying.

XI

Bontsha Speaks

People feel because they are alive: heart beats, lungs take in air, and we feel. Feelings give us the energy to run from danger, to confront mistreatment, to get what we need, to be nourished by what we have, to say good-bye, to start something new. Fear. Anger. Desire. Joy. Sadness. How we respond teaches us about our nature, what we need and want, what we like and dislike, what we can and cannot tolerate, so that we can take appropriate action.

In abusive families children are denied this knowledge as family rules outlaw feelings and self-expression. These rules are made to protect the family secrets, bizarre rules that treat feelings as if they are voluntary, like making it illegal to breathe. But breaking the rules endangers the emotional, and sometimes physical, lives of children in abusive families. In order to survive, we had to follow the rules, though it meant disabling ourselves. Instead of using our energy to feel, express, and act on our emotions, we used it to stifle our feelings. As time goes on, we have more and more unadmitted feelings to suppress. A greater portion of our strength is required to control the energy generated by our hidden emotions. All that underground energy bubbles around, erupting unconsciously even when we believe it is completely under wraps. And we are scared, always scared of what might happen if the whole thing blows.

To become myself, I needed to feel myself. This is what I wanted more than anything. But as I slowly allowed my emotions to surface in therapy, I was terrified of the consequences I'd experienced in my family and my marriage. I talked to Gail about my feelings but I couldn't talk and feel at the same time. I was too afraid my emotions would get out of hand and the result would be rejection, abuse or insanity. Controlling my feelings made me feel safer, though I became aware of how much that control cost me in energy and constraints. I imagined that letting go would happen all at once. I'd either go nuts or be forever free. In fact, feeling and expressing myself was slow, painstaking, stop and go work.

I trusted Gail enough to give her copies of my journal. Because she read them outside our sessions, I was able to distance myself from fear of her reaction. When she didn't respond negatively I trusted her more. I read excerpts and she remained supportive. Rather than reading from my journal, I began to talk about my feelings, though still keeping them under wraps. Gail didn't reject or abuse me. On the contrary, she tolerated and affirmed my feelings, even when I was angry with her. That was a wondrous lesson which I was able to carry out into other relationships. I began to tell my friends how I felt. Although we sometimes quarrelled, I was amazed that my feelings were heard. Gradually I learned to distinguish between people who respected my feelings and those who didn't, opening up more to the ones who did. At the end of my first year in therapy I stopped giving Gail copies of my journal. I trusted her enough to communicate with her directly all the time.

Nevertheless I still put a lot of energy into keeping the lid on myself, especially where my childhood and marriage were concerned. To reduce the pressure of these unexpressed feelings, I worked at letting them out privately. I had a repertoire for releasing old anger: writing, drawing, throwing stones in the woods, dancing, hitting pillows, working with clay. My favourite was my granny doll, which I beat on the floor till her head fell off, then sewed it back on with great glee to bash it again.

The work I did on my own was relieving. I realized I could let out my feelings responsibly. I did not fall apart. I did not go out of control. I did not cry forever. Less of my strength was consumed in suppression. More of my feeling energy was available for living. That energy was unfamiliar. I was just beginning to find out what it could do and how to direct it. Like learning to ride a horse, it frequently left me sore and tired. Sometimes I felt more like the horse was riding me.

Though the work I did on my own was beneficial, it wasn't enough. I wanted to be seen as my emotional self. I wanted the years of silence heard. During my sessions I began to express a little of my anger while feeling it. Gail helped me imagine that the person with whom I was angry sat in her office. This gave me the opportunity to voice what I had wanted to say when I was abused, but couldn't. When I felt the need to release anger physically, I hit a cushion. I wished I could yell but that was still beyond me. I could hardly get out an angry whisper.

It was difficult to let go in front of another person, even someone I trusted as much as Gail. With her witnessing me, my feelings felt deeper, my reality more real. I had mixed reactions. While releasing deeper anger provided the energy I needed to detach myself from the family web, it also revealed new memories, realizations and other feelings, which were often scary and painful. That pain exposed my neediness. It let me know how much I wanted comfort and how much I'd missed it. To show my hurt was risky because in the past my neediness had been used to control and punish me. Asking for comfort meant breaking family rules. It meant risking refusal or the strangeness of consent. But my hurt informed me in no uncertain terms that I couldn't ease my pain alone. It pushed me to chance reaching out as a physical, feeling person. In doing that, I took a vital step toward the caring intimacy I'd never known.

*   *   *   *   *

OCTOBER 26

I understand — my parents had to block their emotions to survive the war. But it really hurts that whether I'm happy and excited, or sad and feeling bad, my parents turn cold, withdrawing from me. When I was little it cut me inside. I learned pretty damn quick to lock up my feelings and never cry.

OCTOBER 28

It's strange. A few days ago I promised myself three things because I was tired of being articulate at the sacrifice of feeling. I promised to hug my feelings close, breathe deep, and let my body be. I'm very physical in my self-expression and I shove my feelings away by holding myself still and tight. Well I'd hardly walked in when Gail said my face looked different and asked me why. I told her and when I had trouble speaking, I explained it was hard for me to talk without pushing away my feelings, and I didn't want to do that. Gail said she'd wait for me. I felt so accepted. It was okay for me to feel and to be unable to speak.

This is the beginning! The door is opening. The sun is waiting. I feel as if I could fly.

OCTOBER 29

I couldn't cry today although I was sad. That scares me. What if all the tears stay inside and choke me? But that won't happen. It won't.

OCTOBER 30

BONTSHA SPEAKS

I understand Bontsha. I know what it's like to be given permission, and believe it, but still be unable to speak except in the merest whisper. I've bowed my head in shame and frustration at my silence, wondering how I ever believed it possible for me to speak. I've heard the bitter laughter of the prosecuting angel. Mama is still triumphant as my fists fall open, rage and tears stifled.

I am angry for Bontsha and all the silent ones. I am angry for myself. I tell you, I'm tired of these mincing little steps, soul bound like the tiny feet of Chinese women before the revolution. I'm tired of the voice raised just a touch, with the quick upward glance to see if it's too loud. I'm tired of admitting the hurt in little doses of "well, I suppose."

How many people did Mama hurt, protected by our silence? And me, yes me, thirty-one years old, and spending more than half my life abused. That's the real picture. Stand back and take a good look at it. I sure as hell have a right to be mad. Come on, open your eyes. I know you can see, you who dream in colour, hear stories in music, shout on paper. Take a good hard look.

See there you are three years old, crouching in a closet until anger turns to fear, and tears give way to nothingness, and Mama takes you by the hand to bed, where if you do right she'll call you a good girl and smile slime that stinks in your heart and burns your dry eyes. See at twenty-three, Eugene hits you with your sins until anger turns to fear, and your tears water his desire, and nothingness becomes sex. Do you see, at three, at twenty-three, your lonely hurt?

Look at you, six and jumping with pride and excitement as Mummy and Daddy drive up with the new baby. She is tiny and perfect, such little hands and little feet. You'll protect her, keep her safe — the shock when they let you hold her and she's so heavy. The shock of suddenly realizing you're little yourself. That's me, the sad little girl, defenseless, a soft-bodied turtle with its shell crushed. I want to be strong, to protect the ones I love from bad things, but I am little and the bad things are squashing me.

I'm eleven, dreaming that I've died and become an angel, announcing to the world that there really is a God and something beyond death, waking up with hope. Crying myself to sleep, I looked within myself for comfort because that was all I had. The sadness of my feeling all alone in the universe.

I am twenty-five and Eugene licks my tears, aroused like a vampire drinking blood. My sadness deepens to despair as I fake him to a come.

That's me, child, girl, woman, always gathering up the remnants of my strength, struggling for warmth, losing myself in the cold, picking up the tatters with numb fingers. That's me, choking and sore, eager to earn "good girl" and a gentle touch, always the hope that I could be loved for myself so small against the belief that I was scum and should be thankful for these small pats.

Look at your life threaded with pain and loneliness. That's how it's been: I was abused.

But see here. Through all of that, you never lost your sense of wonder for the beautiful amazing thing that life is.

I reached out to people who had faith in me: the teacher who sent my poem to the festival and talked to me after school even when I'd moved up a grade, the ones who encouraged me in music, in drama, in writing most of all. Remember Ann ready to come to you at a moment's notice. Think of Rose, hand across the ocean with her letters of encouragement and love, a stranger who owed me nothing but responded to me.

Take a good look at that picture and see yourself. I was abused, I endured, I persevered — not so silently after all because I and no one else elicited the caring of the good people in my life. I and no one else kept alive my sense of beauty and laughter.

Yes I have a right to be angry and a right to be sad and a right to be happy and a right to laugh. Heaven needn't bow its head in shame for me, because I speak. Hey Bontsha, do you hear me? I'm going to speak.

NOVEMBER 6

Gail suggested that if Ted saw her, he might be spurred to get help, which could protect his kids from being abused by him. I haven't been keen on having a session with Ted but if it would help protect my nephews and my niece in any way, then I've got to do it.

NOVEMBER 13

I'm sad. I've been thinking about Gail going on holiday. I'm angry because I hate being left high and dry. It reminds me too strongly of being left to stay with Mama when Mum went to Israel. I felt so betrayed. Endless hell. And when Mum did come home, my long-awaited dream come true, it blew up in my face because I didn't get the comfort I'd yearned for. The hopeless desert of Mama's abuse became permanent. I was terribly lost and sad. I knew then for sure what I'd seen over and over: I was on my own. There was no hope in ever leaning on another person.

Yet here I am, leaning on Gail. When she goes on holiday the prop is withdrawn. I feel like I'm teetering in mid-air — and fear I'll fall flat and hurt myself, realizing I really am alone.

What I have to remember is that Gail's been gone before and returned. It's working through my past that's painful. I find it hard to express my anger and sadness at Gail going away, at the memory of being left alone with Mama. But that's what I have to work at to get beyond it.

The cats are thrilled with my new bed. Snowball is sleeping near my feet and Mitzi beside me. They look so peaceful.

NOVEMBER 16

I'm fed up with therapy. I'm tired of Gail poking around inside my head and stirring things up. I'm no good at anything. Nothing I write will ever be worthwhile. My funk is part tiredness, part pre-teaching jitters and part resurgence of pain I really don't want to face. My head hurts with the effort of keeping it back. My body is in touch with my true self. When I try to run away, various parts of me will hurt or itch or otherwise inform me in a way I can't ignore. See, as I write about it, my headache is starting to go away. The good part is that when I see something beautiful I feel it physically too, as if I'm filled with light sparkling through me. I think the soul is expressed by both body and mind. To separate them is to divide the soul into pieces — which is part of the dilemma of being an incest survivor: having one's soul in scattered pieces so that when part of it is attacked another part can hide in safety. Now I try to find all the pieces and call them back together in unity, reassuring them that it's safe to do so. My bits of soul tentatively approach the centre of my being, ready to bolt at the first sign of danger.

At times I feel that there's something wrong with me because my parents, my brother and sister and their spouses and kids form a family, and I'm outside. At least my parents and I are speaking and we do get along better than we used to. I wonder if we will when I tell them about my grandmother.

Before I go to sleep I just want to say that my hibiscus and my African violets are blooming like mad and my rosebush is coming along nicely.

NOVEMBER 18

I saw *To A Safer Place*, [1] a wonderful film. It awed me to see this woman and members of her family willing to stand up and be counted as survivors. It was an incredible feeling to be part of a large group of people with similar concerns and feelings. It reminded me of the best and worst of group — the elation, the solidarity, the warmth, the strength, the stirred-up garbage and pain. All I want to do today is hide in bed.

This is different from when I was in group because I am aware of my feelings, I can release them by writing. Still I've been depressed, worn-out. Beneath the depression is the feeling that I'm a bad person, that I deserved to be abused. Beneath that is tremendous pain, a howl of outrage that I was so hurt and violated, and a mewling cry of loneliness and sadness.

I'm glad Mary saw the movie with me. I'd have felt lost and lonely afterward if I were by myself.

NOVEMBER 22

I called Ted and asked him to attend a session with Gail. I told him that she thought it was important for my progress. I also told Mum and Dad that I'd called Ted and how important Gail thought a session with him would be. Mum said she was sure Ted would come. I figured they'd dismiss my opinion but respect Gail's as she is the caretaker of the crazy one. I'm hoping that Mum and Dad will apply some pressure on Ted to help his sick sister.

NOVEMBER 24

I feel as if Gail going on holiday scrapes my insides. I know it does me good, but it's hard and feels like shit.

---

1 *To A Safer Place,* a documentary film about Shirley Turcotte, an incest survivor, directed by Beverly Shaffer, National Film Board of Canada, Studio D, 1987.

NOVEMBER 25

USED CAR SALESMEN
Therapists
are socially inclined
used car salesmen.
They hook you in one day
when you're shivering at a bus stop
dreaming of a purring engine and velvet seats.
They don't tell you
about the creaks and leaks,
new parts, rust, weeks in the shop.
When the carburettor
falls through a hole in the bottom
with a crash and gush of oil
and the springs tear through cracked vinyl,
you sit there,
crying in the shop,
wondering how long this time,
remembering with bittersweet laughter
the velvety dream that reeled you
into their practised clutches.
And you pray to God
for the clunk clunk of a working engine
and seats you can sit on.

NOVEMBER 28
It really amazes me that for the first time, I don't see Gail's holiday as an ending. It's a scary, painful event that turns over rocks with slugs underneath. But it's not an ending.

DECEMBER 1
I remember during the summer I turned five being curled up on the living room floor after Mama had hurt me. It was quiet. I thought I was alone. Suddenly I realized Mama had come from nowhere, as if she'd risen up out of the ground. She was bending over me. Mama

asked me what was wrong, as if nothing had happened. Something blew up inside me. I screamed that she had hurt me. She said I was crazy. I kept screaming. She called me a *vilda haye*, a wild animal, and started to hurt me. Though a little voice inside me said very coldly, "Stop this. You're getting hurt. Be quiet," I just couldn't. No matter how much Mama hurt me, I couldn't stop screaming and crying. All the sadness and madness I'd pushed down was exploding out of me. She tried to punch and kick it back inside but it kept jumping out of a different spot.

When Mama threw me into the closet, I sat and tried to hold my breath to keep the feelings from jumping out again. The cold little voice inside me said, "No one is going to help you. Mama runs everything. She's in charge. Mummy went away and she's not coming back, so forget it. You just swallow all that screaming and crying. If you're bad, you're bad. That's the way it is. Just be bad. Don't be anything else. Just bad. Never ever let out all that screaming and crying, or you'll be in big trouble. Nothing will save you." And so that day, waiting for Mama to let me out and take me to her bed, I promised myself I would never scream and cry again.

DECEMBER 8

To allow the child in me to feel and express the painful feelings of long ago, I must trust and depend on Gail. The child part of me is as dependent on her as I was on the adults who betrayed me. I believe that Gail won't let me down the way they did though I'm afraid I have no right to rely on her, no right to expect help and safety. That makes me very, very sad.

DECEMBER 17

It is important that Gail accepts the anger, affection and dependence of the little girl part of me. I've always had to be completely self-reliant. It is a new and amazingly beautiful thing for me to learn that I can be supported by my friends, and support them without being responsible for them; and that it's permissible for me to depend on Gail until the hurt child in me has grown and healed enough to need her no longer; that I'm entitled to feel safe. It's a wonderful thing to be an ordinary person, neither demonically evil nor all-powerful.

DECEMBER 22

Last spring Gail thought I was ready for group again and that because group stirs things up, it would speed up therapy. Well, I didn't want to have any stirring up. My own head was stirring me up as much as I could take. But now I feel ready. There are things I want out of group. I want to talk to other incest survivors about being an incest survivor. I want the solidarity I felt in seeing *To a Safer Place*. I need to truly accept myself as an incest survivor in order to see all of me, the good things as well as the weaknesses. Blocking that full acceptance, thereby masking some of the horror, also blocks my ability to perceive what is good in me. The realization that I am an incest survivor, that I have a right to cry, that I was abused like any of the women in group and that I am not somehow less deserving of anger and sadness, is something that flits in and out of my mind now. I think being in group this time would help me assimilate that awareness.

XII

Caring and Hurting

Though I dealt with other difficult areas, whenever Gail mentioned certain subjects she touched a nerve so raw that I wanted to scream. I was unwilling to talk about her holiday, returning to group, my marriage, dating, seeing her once a week and ending therapy. These subjects had in common one central, excruciating issue: my losses.

My family saw life as a series of losses, a decline that culminated in death. Their view was confirmed by my experience: a history of being stripped away until I had nothing more to give. Gail introduced me to a new view of life: that we give up to get, that endings lead to new beginnings, that this cycle of losses and gains is how we grow. Grieving liberates the energy tied up in denial so it can be used to find peace. We go on as the empty places fill up with living. This view was borne out by my experience in therapy. I found that pain led to progress, giving up my survival mechanisms resulted in better ways of interacting and endings were followed by new beginnings.

When Gail brought up one of the subjects I avoided, she was doing her job: bringing my attention to matters that were holding me back. But I felt so vulnerable, I panicked, retreating into the old familiar view. I could not face my losses because what I'd learned about the grieving process dropped out of sight. I forgot that through grieving I would become free to fill up the emptiness. I believed the emptiness was permanent and unbearable. I must deny it to survive, as I had in my family. I was resentful and angry that Gail brought up these subjects, which caused me such distress. I thought she was trying to make me give up my avoidance, my familiarity, my comfortableness with things as they were. I forgot that this was up to me.

In my family and my marriage giving up was not a matter of choice. They took from me what they could by force, and extorted the rest by threat of abandonment. This surrender never led to anything positive. It facilitated my abuse and led to more surrender. In therapy I discovered a different sort of giving up, one that was voluntary and resulted in a gain. I learned that I could choose my response to losses over which I had no control — like Gail's holiday, gaining something by that response. Giving up my silence over Gail's holiday, for instance, gave rise to valuable feelings and memories.

As my trust in Gail increased and as she continued to bring up these subjects, my terror diminished ever so slowly. I still got angry but I also felt cared for because she took the trouble to confront me. I was able to retain more of my new perspective when I found myself looking at the old view. My new perspective, even if partially blocked, enabled me to consider what I might gain.

I'd thought several times of returning to group in order to please Gail, though never admitting that was my reason. But when push came to shove, I couldn't go through with it and continued to avoid the subject. Watching *To A Safer Place,* however, made me realize that rejoining group could provide solidarity, support and awareness of myself as an incest survivor, which I wanted very much. Once I decided that returning to group was desirable for my own reasons, I was ready to face the losses I associated with it.

Group represented my family to me. I saw myself and the other group members as children, the therapists as parents. When I first began group, I had my sister's support and looked forward to becoming closer with my parents, hoping I could earn my place with them. At the time I returned to group, my sister had abandoned me. My relationship with my parents was strained and I faced the possibility of a total break when I told them about my grandmother. I was aware of how I felt as a child in my family: an outcast, unacceptable, unprotected. I didn't belong in my family and couldn't rely on it. I felt the same way about group: it wasn't dependable and I didn't belong. Though Gail was one of the therapists in group, my trust in her didn't go as far as that. I couldn't imagine her supporting me in group any more than my mother had in my family. I believed Gail, like my mother, was there to care for everyone else but me. I felt scared and alone, the way I did as a child. And my loneliness hurt just as much.

Group evoked feelings and memories around my loss of the caring family I wanted so badly. However, it also presented an opportunity to replay my family life differently, healing my child wounds in the care of responsible adults. In group I found a place where I could practise relating to people honestly while developing my skill in protecting myself. At first I retreated to my cocoon, presenting the outer self remote from me, so I could feel safe. With time, realizing that group was different from my family, I began to come out again as my true self. To my amazement and delight, I gained acceptance, respect and an ability to take care of myself.

1988

JANUARY 3

It's been a wonderful, sleepy day with the phone unplugged. I bought a small flowering cactus and a purple passion vine. I forgot why I hadn't got this plant before — it has smelly flowers. I'll just have to remember to nip them in the bud.

JANUARY 5

What would it be like to be in group and feel a part of it?

JANUARY 6

In the old house I felt I was a part of things. I shared a room with Mum and Dad. Mama couldn't hurt me as long as they were around. I had comforts: the basement, my teddy bear, the next door neighbour. The spring I was in kindergarten, we moved. The toys I loved were all left behind along with my hiding places and the next door neighbour. It was agonizing. I felt as if everything that was good and happy was being cut out of my heart because all I deserved was bad things. I couldn't believe that Mum and Dad would actually take away everything that consoled me and hand me over to Mama.

In the new house I had to share Mama's room. I didn't belong at all any more. Mum and Dad obviously couldn't stand me, to abandon me so totally. They threw me into Mama's corner like dirty underpants shoved in the back of a drawer.

In the new house all the parts of the abuse were concentrated in one nightly act; all Mama's anger compressed into a grenade that exploded while she abused me sexually. There was no release. She came into my bed and I was trapped. They said this was my room, where I belonged. That was my place, between Mama's bed and the wall. So I knew I had no place at all, because I'd never consider my place to be with her.

Mama began to abuse me regularly when I was two, after she returned to live with us. The abuse was still going on when I was nine. I don't know whether it stopped because I became big enough to fight back effectively, or because we stopped sharing a room. She remarried and moved out soon after that.

It's terrible to realize how much longer the abuse lasted than I'd originally supposed. I hate what's being uncovered. It frightens and sickens me. I veil it by thinking I'm an awful person and it was my fault. But it's such a thin, tattered veil. I can see right through to the anger and betrayal and awful sadness beneath.

JANUARY 8

I've called Ted and written him several times now about coming to the city for a session with Gail. Finally he's spoken to her. He's interested in coming to a session, though concerned that the purpose would be for me to tear a strip off him. Gail assured him that it wasn't, although I am angry about his abusing me. He didn't deny the abuse, though he said I blame him for all my problems. Which I don't. He said he would arrange an appointment with Gail as soon as he has an occasion to come to the city. He has a conference coming up in March and we're tentatively planning the session then.

I'd like to talk to Ted about Mama's abuse during this session. I want to tell him before Mum and Dad because he might give me some information about Mama that would be helpful. Once I tell Mum and Dad, Ted will be the good son and say only what they want to hear.

JANUARY 11

Eugene finally called for the things he'd left with me, as well as pots and pans and dishes. I was mad! At the late call and the *chutzpah* (nerve). I only brought what belongs to him. I know that if I start to give it will never end.

I haven't seen him in over a year though he phones periodically and leaves a message on my machine — I don't speak to him. Mary went with me. When I picked her up I felt pale inside. I was shocked by how old and haggard Eugene looked. His eyes were small, bloodshot, glazed. Mary said he reminded her of Charles Manson. Interesting — Ann's husband Rob has said the same thing. Eugene's girlfriend came down just as we were leaving. She looked so young and defenseless, so lost.

I was frightened and sickened by Eugene. I felt dirtied, as though smog had crept into my soul. When I described him to Ann, she said that's how he always looked. He hasn't changed. But now I can see him.

It struck me as pathetic that after so many years and two marriages, all he had left were the few broken things I brought him. I was glad to have Mary's support. Coffee and dessert, walking to a pottery studio, cleansed me of the sickness I felt on seeing Eugene.

My parents insisted I call after I saw Eugene. I did, but Dad was distant and said he'd phone me later. I heard my sister and brother-in-law in the background. I felt as if their concern was a matter of convenience. It reminded me of how isolated I was when I was little and all the distress I felt at seeing Eugene came flooding back. It took tea, talking to friends and a hot bath for me to feel as if I could deal with tomorrow and think again.

JANUARY 12

Rob said that if being a parasite was an Olympic event, Eugene would win a gold medal.

JANUARY 15

How different my apartment is from the days of newspapers piled high, cigarette butts swimming in cold coffee spilt on the floor, t.v.

blaring, the litter smell, no friends, Eugene's shirts crumpled and sweat-stained in the corner, shouts for dinner while I hang up the old grey coat that mortifies me — twice my size and down to my ankles, torn lining leaking fluff; squeezing my way between broken book shelves and garbage to the bathroom, he follows, blowing smoke at me, walls closing in on me.

Now the sun pours in on delicate Chinese evergreen, hibiscus, jade, philodendron rescued from the garage, great green leaves a foot long, yellow freesia in an earthen vase — fragrance fills the room. Tea in a mug Ann gave me, steaming on a solid table that arrived this morning, a triumph from Eaton's at seventy percent off.

Ann dropped by for tea and a chat. She made an appointment for me with a divorce lawyer; I couldn't bear to make the call. Getting divorced reminds me that I was married and how awful it was.

JANUARY 19

I start group again tonight. I'm worn out with fear. I know that shit's going to hit the fan and I'm just waiting for the splatters.

JANUARY 21

CARING

All my life I was under the illusion that I was a giving person. In reality my soul was shut tight inside a closet. I doled out syrup of sympathy through the keyhole to desperate vampires who would suck up any sweet food offered, however devoid of nourishment, helping me to pretend intimacy. It was safe for me in my closet, and it was cold and lonely.

During the last year, parts of me have crept out. I discovered the marvel of being cared for by my friends and caring for them in turn with a bread and milk kind of caring that strengthens our bones. But though the door is open, the little girl in me is still back in that closet, blinking, curious, excited and totally terrified.

The thing about group, you see, is that the intensity burns right through the walls of my closet, exposing the child in me — naked, shivering, by Mama's bed. That child set aside her hurting. She swallowed all her tears and screams. Her parents threw her to Mama like smelly garbage because she was bad. Well, if she was bad, she would be nothing else. She would hold herself still and safe inside that badness. Nothing mattered. She didn't need anybody. If Mummy and Daddy and Ted and Ellen were a family together without her, well that was what she deserved and she had better just live with it. To accept how much it hurt that she had no place at all in the world would have killed her.

So there I am, going on five years old, naked in Mama's room. Suddenly all these people appear — hurt children and adults who say "You don't have to be alone and apart. We understand. We care. You belong here. Let us warm you up with our caring. You don't have to be one little girl alone with a monster. We can lend you our strength to kill it. We'll wash away the ugly pus of your old wounds. We will hold you safe and comfort you."

If I close my eyes, I can pretend that I'm still locked inside my closet and though it's cold and lonely, it's my closet. It is something I know. If I let myself belong and be cared for in this group, then I have to feel the awful sadness and anger at being sacrificed by my parents to my grandmother. I have to feel the despair of being so little and helpless and alone. I have to hold out my arms to be held instead of wrapping them close around my body, and that leaves me open and vulnerable.

When I talked about the incest in group, I couldn't look at anyone because in order to talk about it, I had to imagine myself in nothingness. When I was done talking and glanced around, I saw compassion. Instead of being warm and wonderful, it terrified me. Even now remembering that compassion, I get scared because between that memory and the child in my heart is the fog that shrouds my grandmother's anger. The fog blocks out caring and it holds back the full impact of the abuse from the child I still am. I control the fog. But choosing to allow the caring in, also means choosing to face my grandmother. Will it be different this time? Will I find myself alone with my grandmother, overwhelmed by the awfulness of it, abandoned again? Do I dare believe that I will not be alone, that I will be comforted and warmed?

I want to open my eyes and look around and see myself belonging, cared for, so the child in me can grow up and become strong. But dear God, I am scared.

JANUARY 26

Group is so intense that to keep my sense of proportion I have to maintain a careful balance of fun/work/therapy. Group is like a stomach pump, pumping up the poison. If the poison comes out, it feels awful at first and then relieving. But when I push the poison back down, the two opposing pressures make me feel like I want to die.

JANUARY 27

While talking in group, one of the women made faces that reminded me of Mama. I started to shake, not realizing why at first. I thought of the stomach pump pushing up the poison. As it pushed I was shaking harder. It would be awful to go home like that. So I spoke up. Gail helped me express the feelings about Mama that had surfaced. She didn't let go. When I felt as if I was sliding into the past, she reminded me that I am an adult and the slide stopped. I felt protected on both sides by Gail and the other therapist, Anna. Afterward I was shaky and wanted to giggle, elated with relief.

JANUARY 29

Sometimes when Mama abused me, I removed myself to her curtains, imagining that I'd wrapped them around me, safe in a protective tunnel. Mostly I hid inside myself, feeling as if she was hurting someone else. I tried to be quiet and unreal because when I was present, she often hurt me worse. It was safer to be unreal but there was a part of me that couldn't stay gone. It pushed through all my fear, all my wisdom of self-protection, and made me be myself from time to time.

JANUARY 30

Dad and Mum have been in the city for a convention. Dad and I went for a walk after dinner. We discussed the changes in my life, my marriage, why I became a C.A., writing, being a child at heart, growth, the process of life. It was a good talk. I was myself and Dad spoke about his feelings. He brought up a time we were arguing about Eugene. I recall it differently, but Dad thinks I said I hated him. He started to cry. I hugged him and cried too. I reminded him of all the times I've told him how much I love him, how special he is to me. I wish he could remember that.

Dad referred to a discussion I had with Ellen last spring, about remembering. At that time I felt stuff churning inside me but didn't have any actual memories of Mama abusing me. I told Dad I had been abused for a number of years by someone before Ted. I wasn't ready yet to discuss it, I said, but planned to talk to him and Mum about it in the spring. Dad didn't show any reaction to that though he asked me whether it had anything to do with him or Mum. I said no.

Dad told me that he and Mum consulted a psychologist but they felt that if they had counselling, they'd open a can of worms that was forty years old and older, from their childhoods as well. At this stage of their lives, they can't handle spending the next few years dealing with that kind of pain. I'm glad that I won't ever have to be scared of the worms. The can is open. I'm looking at and touching the awful wormy mess, putting it to rest. Then I can live my life fully, without fear of what I might find within myself. I'll know the good and the bad. I'll be able to be myself without the weight of the secrets dragging me down. My soul will unfold and fly.

Dad said that when Ellen was talking to me, I made her sick by mentioning the abuse. He told me how sick he and Mum get. I tried to explain that I feel hurt and isolated because no one in the family can talk to me about the abuse, about my feelings and theirs. Yet I understand.

"If you understand, how can you be hurt?" he asked.

I said, "Look, I'm not asking you to change. You don't even have to understand. I just want you to accept that although I know you can't handle anything to do with the abuse, I feel hurt and isolated."

"I accept there is no logic to it," Dad said. "It is crazy and nothing we say matters."

I think he understood a little bit when I said that if he were hungry and went to the store, he would not stop being hungry just because the store was closed.

After Dad and I got back to the hotel, Mum said she was angry at my negative reaction to her comment that Mama told nice stories. Mama wasn't there to defend herself, she said. I made Mum look like a weakling and it wasn't true, she never let Mama interfere. I was angry because she let Mama interfere all right. But all I could think of was "not now. Not this, now." So I told her that I'd like to discuss Mama with her in the future, during a session with Gail. For the time being if she didn't want me to say anything negative about Mama, she should just not mention her. That's how we left it. But there I go, ruining things again.

I'm the bad one and I'm going to be worse. Coming home, I thought of changing my mind, not telling them about Mama. But I need to do that for me. They've decided they want to leave the can of worms closed. That's fine for them. But I'm just thirty-one. I want to spill all those worms out and get rid of them. And part of that is spilling out the secret of Mama.

I feel like a worm myself and I wish I were dead. I think Mum and Dad would be better off. Ted and Ellen would be relieved. Yet I remember when we said good-bye, how Dad hugged me tight. He said he loved me and told me to take care. In his face, his hugging, his voice, was all the caring he can't give me because of his can of worms shut tight. I don't want to be the blight any more, the sickness, the poison. It hurts too much.

FEBRUARY 1

I had a wonderful time celebrating my debt-free status with friends last night. After everyone left I felt so peaceful, full of good food and friendship.

FEBRUARY 5

I'm very, very sad, bowed down by the sorrow of the little girl I was. I want to be comforted. I crave gentle, non-sexual touching. I get it from my friends and cats, but it's not enough. Will my needs ever be met or is there always going to be that deep wound?

FEBRUARY 14

THE HURTING
I wanted to come to a place
where I could be feel real
and I feel real
all of me holding
hands bowing heads
hurting rocking torn
from the silence

wordless hurt
images
of group
and Mama,
a house pain alone

Here
I am
real the images are
horrible truths
and all of me holding
hands for comfort and strength
voices the hurting.

FEBRUARY 17
I talked about the hurting in group. Gail asked how they could help me with my sadness. It was terribly hard, but with much shaking and struggle I said I'd like a hug. It felt good and I'm really glad of it.

The hurting is so big. Letting it out little by little helps, but at times I can't look beyond it.

MARCH 5

What an absolutely beautiful day! Last night I had a wonderful set of thoughts that left me breathless. I'm not sure I can absorb it yet.

I was thinking about the stories I made up when I was little — stories for my friends, for Ellen, just for myself. The stories were about all kinds of things — adventure, fantasy, fable — funny and serious. I thought, here was this little kid who was being abused still able to make up stories, something creative and good growing in me despite the shit. It's not only the stories. I remember being the leader in our games, singing on the bus, running down hills as if I had wings.

I've told Gail how I skipped class and daydreamed when I was a teenager. But I forgot about saving babysitting money for four years so I could travel the summer I graduated from high school. I forgot about performing in a play and folk dancing. I forgot about tramping through the woods taking photographs for a biology class. I forgot about skiing and sending off stories to magazines. I forgot about fun math and tutoring.

The memory of myself as a child was a cold, broken thing. It is becoming whole. As well as sadness and withdrawal, I see vitality, creativity, involvement. I feel compassion and liking for myself, a peacefulness settling inside me.

XIII

I Can See It

As children in abusive families, we tried to minimize the abuse and earn the caretaking we needed by complying with our parents' demands, both spoken and non-verbal. To satisfy them, we assumed the characteristics we thought they wanted us to have, characteristics which became our roles. To avoid abuse and neglect, we suppressed or disguised what didn't fit these roles. Parts of us went underground, disconnecting from our external selves, and remaining undeveloped. Splitting ourselves in hidden pieces enabled us to survive, but cost us dearly.

After I left Eugene, I split off the part of me that had been his wife, removing myself emotionally from the horror of my marriage. It was a difficult task to embrace that part of myself. When I met Eugene I was an adult living on my own. I was not a helplessly dependent child. I chose to be with him. I chose to stay. And I blamed myself for every horrible thing he did to me because of those choices.

To let go of blame for my marriage, I had to realize that the neglect and abuse I'd experienced in childhood had kept me from growing up. I was, in fact, helplessly dependent. Contrary to possessing woman-of-iron invulnerability, I was terribly vulnerable. Nobody taught me how to protect myself. Being defenseless and open to abuse was all I knew, so that a man who was evil and manipulative could make mush of me. I chose to stay, a choice made in ignorance, pain and weakness. I also chose to build up my strength, getting what I needed so I could leave Eugene. To give myself credit for that accomplishment, I had to recognize how far I'd come, admit how dominated and abused I had been. That admission was painful. I blunted the pain with my guilt, minimizing Eugene's betrayal. To be capable of true intimacy, I needed to forgive myself as I confronted the reality of my marriage.

I also split off my relationship to my grandmother and my brother, thinking of them as boarders who happened to live with me. As strangers, their betrayal didn't seem so bad. I could ignore the pain I felt over the loss of their love. To maintain the illusion of our non-relationship, I cut off any part of me that resembled my abusers, in the same way I cut off feelings and experiences that reminded me of the abuse. This separation was brutal, as if I were sliced in pieces by shards of ice. I felt divided, at war with myself. Admitting my close relationships to Eugene, my brother and my grandmother revealed the full extent of their betrayal. But as I dealt with the pain it caused me, the ice melted. I was becoming a whole person, at peace with myself.

*   *   *   *   *

MARCH 11

Belonging means letting go of the toughness, the belief that "I don't need anyone," allowing myself to look at the peaceful place in me. I imagine it as a house on an island, a place of trees, meadows, lakes, birds and cats; also spots that have been strip mined, the land raw and ugly where I was abused. I have to go to those spots and mourn until I'm cried out. Then I can sit peacefully and soak up the healing sun.

MARCH 16

Though my grandmother died a few months before I started therapy, she's still a part of my life. The painful realization I've grappled with for the last few days is that I *am* connected to my grandmother. My effort to separate myself from her has also separated me from my past, my family past and the past of my people. It has disconnected me from important aspects of myself. Gail said today that I, *like my grandmother*, am a storyteller. It's true, my grandmother was. It makes me want to cut this piece out of my heart, yet how can I do that, it's such an important part of me. I won't stop writing again.

How can it be that the woman who beat me and used me like garbage also gave me part of what is most precious to me? I've cried a lot in the last few days and especially today. If I thought it was hard to acknowledge the negative ways in which I am like my grandmother, it was nothing to the pain of acknowledging the positive connection between us. It makes me feel the betrayal as a knife in my heart.

MARCH 17

What a weird dream. I'm still a bit out of breath.

I dreamt that I was having a session with Gail. There were four or five bunches of flowers and plants in the room. I imagined that they represented different aspects of myself. Each one had a song. The prayer plant was my fear. One plant was vibrantly coloured, black and purple and other colours. I told Gail it was singing a belt song, "I Can See It." It was the part of me that is strong and courageous. Then Gail said, "What about those?" I hadn't noticed them before. They were tall white gladioli. I didn't want to talk about them. I said, "It's just a fancy," but Gail wouldn't let me get away with that. Then I was on the floor and the white flowers were out of the jug, crawling toward me. Gail had her hand on my back. I curled into a ball. Gail kept asking "What about those?" The flowers became Mama, Gail disappeared, and I stopped breathing. I woke up breathless.

MARCH 25

I've been crying a lot, and I find it comforting to cry with my teddy bear. All the tension leaves my body and I just cry.

MARCH 26

I feel alone and unloved. Eugene called again about his yearbooks, which are supposedly missing from the stuff I brought him. Hearing from him is enough to put anyone off.

APRIL 1

It's spring in my mind — all kinds of things popping up all over the place, and especially things I've been avoiding, my marriage for one. I bought a new vacuum cleaner. The old upright just blew dust around. This new one is fantastic. It works!

APRIL 5

It's hard talking about my marriage. I feel very vague, like I did when I first started talking about the abuse in my childhood.

I've called Mary a couple of times to ask her if she wants me to mail the cheque for the work she did for me or if she wants to pick it up. I left messages twice but she didn't return my calls. Is something wrong?

APRIL 6

Mary answered the phone this time. I asked her if she was angry, avoiding me, and she said yes.

She is resentful because she feels I don't accept where she's at. She gave me two examples. Some months ago I was talking to a friend of hers about abuse. Mary asked, "Don't you think sometimes the victim is responsible, instigates it?" I said no. Mary then referred to herself, beaten by her mother, as an example of a victim bringing it upon herself. I said that Mary's mother was the one responsible.

The other example was when Mary told me that in her experience, happiness is always accompanied by pain. I said that I experience happiness on its own, though I have in the past felt happiness mixed with pain. I wondered if Mary might not someday feel happiness and pain separately.

I'm all a muddle. I feel angry, hurt, helpless, scared. I want to run away.

APRIL 8

I tossed and turned, thinking about what Mary said. Am I overbearing and bossy without realizing it? Ann and Alma say no. I couldn't be silent when she said the victim contributes to abuse; I would betray myself. What can I do differently? Mary won't tell me if she's angry or disturbed by something I say. She says she can't. She wants me not to say upsetting things. I turned myself into a pretzel to please Eugene, Ruth, others. But I'll go crazy if I change to please everyone.

I'm pissed off. I thought our friendship was open and aboveboard. I don't like being avoided. I feel yucky, thinking of how she hugged me and acted nice while she was angry with me. I don't want to wonder about the unsaid things underneath.

I keep thinking that Mary and I have been good friends for over a year. There should be enough to keep the friendship going; is this another case of getting too close too fast?

APRIL 12

Mary and I have met and talked. I like Mary a lot but I'd rather see the end of our friendship than change to please her. That's different, isn't it!

APRIL 15

For the last week and a half I've been dreaming about Eugene several times every night. Talk about being tired.

Thinking about my dreams, it seems to me my sleeping self is saying that I can't just take Eugene out of my life. I have to face and deal with my marriage, though it's okay to cry about it. I've been crying on and off all day, feeling sad. Angry too. But mostly sad.

NEED

I've protected myself from the reality of my marriage in the same ways I protected myself from the reality of my childhood abuse, both during and after: numbness, guilt, oblivion, busyness, forgetting, minimizing.

I understand that it replicated the abuse I experienced as a child — even the link between physical and sexual abuse paralleled my grandmother's treatment of me. But that intellectual understanding doesn't create the emotional connection that's missing between the person I am now and the person I was just a short time ago. There's a gap between the woman I was at twenty and the woman I am. My marriage is in that gap. It is the bridge between my past and my present and I can't be myself, all of myself, without crossing that gap.

I've said my marriage could have been worse — I could have married a wife-beater. But Eugene did beat me. He didn't break any bones, true, but being whipped and hit with a belt or the butt end of a whip is physical abuse.

I've said that my marriage could have been worse, I could have married an alcoholic. It's true that Eugene didn't drink, but he lied, was unreliable, couldn't work, couldn't get along with people and acted inappropriately in many social situations. I covered up for him and made excuses for him. I can't count the times I went out in the middle of the night because he'd run out of coffee or cigarettes, frantically looking through pockets for enough change because we'd also run out of money. I was afraid we'd be evicted because Eugene screamed at me so often in the middle of the night. So I don't really see how it could have been much worse.

I've said that at least Eugene didn't humiliate me in public. But he embarrassed me in front of my friends and clients by being obviously sullen, dominating the conversation, being belligerent, talking either about sexual oddities or impending doom and claiming expertise where he was ignorant. All that besides the times he yelled at me in public; besides the times I had to wear clothes that embarrassed me; besides the times Eugene fondled my breasts while we waited for the bus.

I didn't want to be abused, frightened and humiliated. I felt like I was going crazy. But as long as I could stand it, I did. It's difficult for me to see myself in that light — as a woman who allowed herself to be abused. It doesn't fit with the woman-of-iron image I've always had of myself.

Though I hate Eugene, though I'm angry with him, though he disgusts me, I can feel compassion for him because he must be a thoroughly frightened, empty person. I feel sad that I believed I deserved no better than to be abused and used by him. But I don't like the need that kept me in my marriage. The awful thing is that I don't feel the compassion for myself that I feel for Eugene. And truly, I think I deserve it more than he does. After all, I don't make a career out of being a tapeworm.

I read the story "Need" for the first time in early adolescence. I've reread it countless times. It haunted me, even though the character that drew me to the story wasn't particularly likeable. He sensed other people's needs as a physical pain which could only be eased by satisfying the need. He wasn't a nice person, he was simply compelled, driven to satisfy people's wants because of the distress their neediness caused him.

It struck me recently that I've been haunted by this story because it described my reaction to needy people — not necessarily the most helpful response, but a compulsion to stop the neediness. Yet if I could have filled someone's needs, what use would I be once they were met? I'd have been revealed as the worthless being I knew I was. The solution was to find someone whose needs were endless. Eugene was perfect. No matter how much I gave it wasn't enough, he wanted more, until he nearly consumed all that I was.

That makes me think of the last thing I've said about my marriage. I liked to believe that if I hadn't married Eugene, I would have married someone else just like him. It's as if by being certain that I was waiting for someone exactly like Eugene, I can deny that he had any effect on me — because after all it was what I wanted. There's a grain of truth there. I did want distraction from my internal pain and confusion and I got plenty of distraction from Eugene. But my marriage did change me. I don't know just how, but you can't be gradually squashed for nearly ten years, you can't let go of everything you hold dear and accept everything abhorrent, without being changed.

Since I separated from Eugene, I've found so much of myself, again. I have 110 items on the list of how I see myself. I rediscovered my writing, my love of music, my awe of life, all the things that were ground down while Eugene and I were together. Somehow I hoped I could go back to being the person I was and forget that my marriage ever existed. But the person I was married Eugene. The person I was believed that I was horrible and worthless. I wondered at being alive, despaired of really living, denied my right to feel and was overwhelmed by pain I couldn't understand. Those 110 items weren't me when I was twenty. They are the me I am now, the me that is becoming. I wouldn't want to go back to being the girl who valued herself so little that she threw herself under Eugene's feet. Maybe I do feel some compassion for her because, despite her strength and imagination and warmth, she was depressed; and in the terrible gloom of depression even Eugene could look good.

THREE

End

XIV

Authority

Those of us abused in our families were victims of their authority. We learned much about misuse of power, but little about authority used beneficially to guide, set appropriate limits, protect, teach, supervise, encourage and let go. We missed important information on dealing with authority constructively: how to benefit from good authority, safeguard ourselves from bad, and tell the difference between them.

In my family authority was embodied by my grandmother. She used the power of her age and position to make us service her emotionally, physically and sexually. Unlike my grandmother, my parents did use their authority to help us, giving as much guidance as they could. But this help was limited by their own lack of independence. Rather than moving us toward autonomy, their authority was geared to control us. My brother's authority over me came from his hero role in the family and his age. Like my grandmother, he used his position to sexually abuse me.

Given what I'd learned, it's not surprising I wanted to stay away from authority. I believed I could help myself better than anyone else, and in my family that was certainly true. I thought there was only one type of authority and it was abusive. In my family that was also generally true. I survived that authority by keeping my distance as much as I could. Because my anger was forbidden, I channelled its energy into resentment of authority, an acceptable outlet that fit my role as the family rebel.

As I grew older and came into contact with other authority figures, the attitudes that had been protective in my family became detrimental. I had no idea how to tell the difference between good and abusive authority so I could defend myself or get help as needed. I was proud of my rebellious attitude toward authority. I thought it reflected my independence. It actually showed how isolated I was, unable to reach out for help because I was too scared and ignorant. I had great faith in my own authority but little idea of where it belonged. I didn't know how to evaluate it because my views of my age, strength, knowledge and position were distorted. I rated my powers either too high or too low. I often gave up my authority when it was rightfully mine and defiantly clung to it when I'd have been better off guided by someone else.

Entering therapy meant asking for help from an authority figure. This terrified me, although there were positive experiences that countered my fear. Memories of encouraging teachers and respectful supervisors provided the springboard I needed to take a chance on my therapist. With Gail I experienced a longer term, deeper relationship which taught me the difference between good and bad authority. Learning how to guard and how to let people across my boundaries, I discovered I could protect myself from authority, profit from it, outgrow it and go on. I came to respect my own authority, realizing it develops throughout my life in the way I use it and in what I learn from others.

1988

APRIL 21

Last night I dreamt that Gail was helping me fold laundry. It surprised me because folding laundry is so mundane and personal, as opposed to therapeutic. Gail said she was in a bad mood. I told her I couldn't imagine that. She asked why, which set me at ease because it was more like therapy. I told Gail that I saw her in an exalted position. I could imagine her languishing but not in a bad mood like an ordinary person.

Then I became quite conscious that I was cutting the dream short. It wasn't a bad dream. On the contrary, it was interesting and I had the feeling that something good would be revealed, but for some reason I had to cut it off.

Before falling asleep I wondered why I have so much trouble knowing what I want from Gail and taking compliments from her. Why am I startled when she says she's thought about me or is glad of something I've said? Why do I dream about bad things happening to me as a result of her giving to me? Why do I dream that I must give to her when I don't want to?

I believe what came next in my dream was how things would be different if I weren't holding myself back to keep some distance from Gail. I started therapy with a barrier, a fence, between me and Gail as Authority. The fence guarded me from the misuse of authority, which I remembered and feared from childhood. It also filtered out some of her support as it passed through the barrier. My fence served me well because it made me feel safe. Viewing Gail as "exalted" protected me from the risks of personal interaction. But it kept a lump of ice in my heart. I want a different way to view our relationship. I don't need a barrier any more. I trust Gail. The fence doesn't suit me.

APRIL 22

I talked to Gail about the fence. She said this is the beginning of the end of therapy. I get so scared and sad, by turns. I feel filled up with tears. I'd like to go to bed for a week.

I have a clear idea of what comes next. It's as if in my left hand I have good memories, good endings, love, warmth, gifts from the people in my life, past and present. In my right hand are the unhealed hurts, the bad endings and abuse. In each hand is a glacier that's been gradually receding. There is ice between my two hands, keeping them apart and me from being whole. The ice has kept the pain at bay, and the good things as well. As the glaciers have receded, I've been taking more of the pain and good things into myself, but am still divided. Now it's time for the ice between to melt, for the left hand to clasp the right. When I was little Mum called me a fire. How did she know? When my fingers touch, embers burst into flame, love leaps from hand to hand and grief crackles through my soul. Out of that burning, I grow.

APRIL 27

Bruno Bettleheim, from *Surviving* [1] writing about how Holocaust survivors handle survivorship:

> One group of survivors allowed their experience to destroy them; another tried to deny it any lasting impact; and a third engaged in a lifelong struggle to remain aware and try to cope... (p. 28)

The first type of survivor believes:

> it should be the special obligation of the family (or of the community) to take care of him because he had suffered incredibly, and was unable to do it himself. It is the tacit request and expectation that others ought to solve his problems for him... (p. 30)

The second way of handling survivorship requires defenses, which were:

> mainly repression and denial. In consequence, their integration is somewhat shaky and incomplete — because a most important group of feelings is denied access to awareness — and their personalities are to some degree depleted of energy for coping realistically with life, since they must expend it on keeping repression and denial going ... their life is full of inner insecurity. (p. 31)

The third type of survivor:

> tried to salvage something positive from their ... experience — horrible as it had been. This often made their lives more difficult than their old ones had been, also in some ways more complex, but possibly even more meaningful. This is the advantage they

---

1   Bruno Bettleheim, *Surviving and Other Essays* (New York: Vintage Books, New York, 1980).

derived from ... [giving] full cognizance to the most tragic experience of their lives ... A precondition for a new integration is acceptance of how severely one has been traumatized, and of what the nature of the trauma has been ... Personal integration, and with it achievement of meaning, is a highly individual, lifelong struggle. (pp. 34–36)

Isn't this all familiar? I've known incest survivors of the first type who subsist on therapy, looking for the saviour who will take their needs away, but of course they're always disappointed. They bewail their situation but never accept the possibility of improving it in any way, however small. I've known the second type too. I was one till I started therapy. I remember very well how much energy went into keeping the shadows at bay, the necessary numbness. Now I'm struggling on the third path. There must be some meaning, something positive, something greater than the horror in my experiences. If nothing else, I am who I am as a result of what I've been through and as a result of the struggle to become wholly myself.

I've started dealing with my marriage in therapy, and it's hard. Eugene was as abusive as my grandmother but I was an adult in my marriage. It's hard for me to give myself the freedom to feel the pain and anger that's burbling to the surface. Somehow I doubt that I'm entitled to hate Eugene, since I chose to stay with him (though Ann says everybody else hated him, why shouldn't I, who had more reason to?). I'm afraid to express my feelings for Eugene aloud, though I've started to, tentatively, because it is a final admission that I was badly hurt. I keep thinking of what Bettleheim said: that I've got to accept the severity of the hurt I experienced living with Eugene, to realize that I'm changed by it and to find the meaning.

I was so utterly squashed in my marriage and yet was able to become unsquashed. There must be a pretty strong life force inside me to do that. I'll never forget what it was like to be a living death, and I'll never allow *any* part of myself to be squashed by *anyone* again. And if I can do something, however small, to give someone else a boost out of squashedness, I think that's the best thing I could do with my life.

APRIL 30

Hurray!!! I'm done with tax season!! Tomorrow Alma and I are going to the ballet and then we're meeting Ann and her mother for coffee afterward. I love the ballet, and it's ages since I've been. We're seeing two modern pieces. One is called "Song of the Earth," about the cycle of life and rebirth. The other is an exploration of emotions called "Voluntaries."

MAY 2

I alternate between anxiety and being sick to my stomach. The horribleness of my marriage hits me in waves. Thank God, I'm out of it.

Eugene got off on forcing me to express desire for what I loathed. He had to keep changing the rules so he could continue to enjoy the thrill of dominating me in a cruel, warped way. What a sick, disgusting man. I hate his guts.

MAY 9

I've always had trouble with authority figures. I resented other people's rules, which I was good at bending and from which I ran when I couldn't bend them to suit me. I've kept my distance from authority. But something occurred to me last night while I was lying in bed. Authority does not have to be the king of the castle, power and domination. It can be the imparting of wisdom, like a wisewoman who teaches, dispensing herbs and knowledge. I wonder about my own authority. Will it be rejected or acknowledged? Facing authority, my own and others', means removing barriers, opening to greater love and greater grief.

MAY 11

I saw *Irma LaDuce*[2] on Saturday. It was entertaining but it hurt me where I'm raw. The whole idea of Irma believing that she should

---

2 *Irma LaDuce*, a feature length musical comedy about a French prostitute and the man who falls in love with her, directed by Billy Wilder, United Artists, 1963.

whore and support her pimp, that anything else is inappropriate and belittling, her inability to receive caring from a lover, reminds me of myself in my marriage. I think there's a part of me that feels like a whore. Eugene used me like one and I feel as if I sold myself to keep him.

When I got home there was a message from Mum. She said the Mother's Day card was beautiful and she liked what I wrote even better. It made her feel glad and touched. That made me feel very good too. I wrote, sincerely, that I chose the card because it was warm, sunny and beautiful, and so reminded me of Mum. Also that Ann, on seeing old photos, said that Mum and I look like two peas in a pod — and I'm glad we do.

MAY 15

I have to say that Mum was better than her mother. She tried her best to be different from Mama. While it's true I was abused, Mum gave me skills that helped me cope, survive and grow, like a love of reading. While she was ironing she'd say, "Don't you iron. Buy permapress. It's better to read a book than iron." She told me it was better to read than cook, better to read than clean, and I could see her pleasure, reading in bed at night, which I did too.

MAY 17

I spoke to a woman in group tonight who has been venting her anger by picking on women's weak spots. I said that when she is angry, she lashes out at people in a cruel way and I don't like it. Her behavior does remind me of Mama and Eugene, but I felt that what I said came not as a reaction to triggers from the past, but because I don't like what she is doing here. I'm glad I was able to speak out although she frightens me.

I've asked Mum and Dad to meet with me and Gail when Dad comes to the city on business, June 2. I plan to tell them then about Mama abusing me.

MAY 21

Telling Mum and Dad about Mama will bury the corpse of my childhood. I've got to grow up without ever having had a real childhood. That's just the way it is.

It's hard to believe that ending therapy will be different from when I was little, forced into adult burdens before my time. It's hard to trust that Gail will not kick me out before I'm ready.

MAY 23

A conversation with Mum:

Me: "Dad told me you were apprehensive about seeing Gail because you don't want to talk about Mama. I know it would be difficult for you, but I'd like you to come anyway."

Mum: "I'm sorry, but it's my prerogative to choose not to come."

Me: "That's true, but you've said you'd like to help, and I'd like you to come."

Mum: "I won't hear anything bad about Mama. She's not here to defend herself. I can't confront her the way I did Ted. Anyway, you imagined it. I spoke to a psychologist and she said it's between you and your therapist. It has nothing to do with me."

Me: "Yes it does because you didn't protect me."

Mum: "I've thought and thought and I don't recollect anything. Mama was good to you and loved you."

Me: "That's what you believe, but it's not true. If you could recollect something, you would have protected me."

Mum: "It's between you and your therapist. Let her talk to the psychologist I spoke to. I'm not going to come."

MAY 25

In group tonight I talked about Mama. Gail helped me speak as the four-year-old I'd been. I was shaking, hurt and sick, remembering how Mama looked so big and monstrous. Gail sat across from me on the floor. That made me feel safe and warm and she rubbed my back when I cried. The understanding and compassion of the other women in group was a wonder to me. I was able to ask Gail for a hug and it felt good. I saw the affection and caring in her face. That made me feel very good.

JUNE 2

I'm petrified about tomorrow. Dad and I are meeting with Gail and I'm going to tell him about Mama. We had a lovely time this evening. We had dinner and went for a long walk, discussing things and the price of them. It was great.

I talked to Dad about writing and he understood perfectly. He told me that Michelangelo described working in stone as releasing the figure that was inside, and it could only be what it was. Dad said, like Michelangelo, one can only write what is inside. I gave him copies of two poems which he read and said were beautiful.

JUNE 5

It's funny. If things had gone badly when I told Dad on Friday about Mama abusing me, I'd probably have written about it right away. I've been so stunned and exhausted by things going well that I'm just getting around to writing about it now.

Dad believed me!!! His initial reaction was that it was incomprehensible. Not that he disbelieved me, but that it didn't fit Mama's character as he knew it. Gail asked him if he'd seen a negative side to Mama and he said no. But afterward he told me that he was against Mum discussing Mama with me because she'd had an absolutely horrible time with Mama, going way, way back, and if she rooted around in the past she might uncover all sorts of things. He was afraid she'd have a nervous breakdown. He gave me the impression of secrets in Mum's life that might be exposed and which she couldn't handle.

Dad was sympathetic, supportive, concerned. He said, "Poor Lily. It must be horrible to have memories like that of your grandmother." I told him that as a child I'd been too scared to tell on Mama. Dad's response was, "Of course, you were terrified." I hugged him and he patted my back. I said, "I love you so much." He understood how difficult and painful it was to remember and deal with the abuse. I told him I'd stayed with Eugene because, however awful it was, it seemed like all I deserved. He asked what he could do to help. I said that all I'd wanted was for him to say he was sorry that I'd been so hurt, and he'd given me that. He cried then, and I hugged him. He asked if I'd be able to put this behind me. I answered yes, though it would always be a part of me. Gail pointed out that my being able to tell him showed how far I'd come, though I still had work to do.

Dad said he hoped I'd be able to get closer to the family. I told him that it depended in part on whether I was accepted. I used the analogy of him, as a Holocaust survivor, trying to be close to someone who didn't believe the Holocaust had occurred.

We had coffee together afterward. Dad was so warm and loving and concerned. I still can't absorb it.

He also told me that if you don't want to believe something, the easiest thing to do is to say it was imagined or dreamed. He was talking about Mum and her reaction. I understood.

Dad said he was glad I'd told him, that it must be a load off my mind.

It's a funny thing. I should be ecstatic, but I'm not. Dad's response on Friday was like a dream come true. But I'm scared and sad. I feel adrift, pulled in different directions.

XV

Childhood's End

Rather than living authentic lives, my family was engaged in acting out a play. The reality of abuse, neglect, and exploitation was hidden behind our act. Airing unspoken conflicts in backhanded ways, we played the close, loving family who kissed and hugged up a storm. My parents played the parts of good man and good woman: he was supposed to be logical and silent while she was emotional and intuitive. My brother and sister were the good boy and girl. He was smart, she was popular. They grew up to carry out my parents' dreams of accomplishment: my brother as a doctor, my sister married to one; he an observant Jew, she a corporate success. My role provided an explanation for family tensions, a diversion from the real problems.

To hide the abuse, present the loving front and act out all the unspoken feelings and conflicts, our roles were many-sided and intricately entangled. Complex as they were, however, our roles were rigid. There was no place for our true personalities. There was no recognition of change and growth. When I kept kosher (religious dietary laws), it was a crazy thing to do, yet it was admirable when my brother did. Since they weren't natural, these roles required a nonstop effort. We were always on show. My brother could not become religious enough nor my sister successful enough to relax.

Exposing my brother's abuse was not in the script. For telling the truth, I was treated with coldness until the script could be repaired. "Incestuous assault" was called "childhood experimentation," and all went on the way it used to. My brother's role as pious doctor, husband and father was restored. My part got smaller as I rejected this deception. Contact with my parents was often strained, limited to discussing the weather. They hoped someday I'd come back into the family fold as before, while I hoped that someday I'd come into the fold as myself.

With the right conditions and persistence, a natural transformation process occurred. Encouragement, guidance and safety allowed feelings and thoughts to emerge at a tolerable pace. I slowly learned to distinguish between my reality and the family script.

With Gail I practised being who I was instead of acting the way I was supposed to. I applied what I learned to other relationships, gradually replacing my role with the real me. Through finding acceptance in group, I learned that all families weren't alike. Because the group "family" did not reject me, I realized that I could belong, and did belong, first and foremost by being connected with my real self, and then by connecting to other people.

I couldn't be true to myself and play a role at the same time. While I kept my grandmother's secret, a part of me was acting in the family play. I was a fragmented person, pulled in different directions by the reality I accepted with one face and the role I played with another. To become whole, I had to quit the lie. By exposing my grandmother's abuse, I forced a change. I risked losing my family but I gained my integrity.

My brother wasn't going to give up his role for reality. Ted had a strong stake in the family deception, as it minimized his abuse. We hadn't had any contact since the early spring when he cancelled our tentative date for a session with Gail. I preferred it that way. Out of sight, out of mind — my sense of betrayal at my brother's hands lay dormant as long as I didn't speak to him.

My sister stopped talking to me after I brought Ted's abuse into the open and disclosing my grandmother's abuse didn't bring her any closer. I had high hopes of a relationship with Ellen because she was the one member of my family who hadn't abused me in my childhood. My hopes were crushed when she cut me off. I couldn't accept her rejection. Buying the family myth that she was "normal," I expected more from her than my parents. I didn't realize she was as driven by the script as the rest of the family. Bearing the burden of my family's idea of "normal," she was supposed to be a combination of June Cleaver, Kathleen Turner and Margaret Thatcher. In her mid-twenties, she was a vice-president running a five-bedroom house. There was no room to deal with incest.

My mother's position was clear: the script must be upheld. I was angered and hurt by her reaction, but not surprised. I imagined she had memories of her own that would be tough to handle if they were triggered by my experiences. I knew how painful it would be for her to deal with her own mother's betrayal. Despite her insistence that she would not talk about my grandmother, my mother did discuss the abuse with me in a roundabout way, and I was grateful. I knew our relationship would be affected by my telling the secret. What that would mean to me or how I'd feel about it remained to be seen. I didn't realize then how much my mother was ready to extend herself to preserve both her view of my grandmother and some connection with me.

My father was willing to hear what I had to say, accepting me as I really was. At first. Hug and punch was a typical pattern in my family but I wasn't consciously aware of that. All my life I'd been taken in by the hug, wanting it so much I was shocked by the punch. I underwent the hug and punch when I told my parents about my brother's abuse: my father so sympathetic he cried, the next day icy cold; my mother sharing her fears and experience of sexual abuse only to deny it in anger soon after. Though I was warmed by my father's support, I felt uneasy with it, unconsciously bracing myself for the punch.

I had grieved all my life without realizing it: the times I felt sad, without knowing why, the times I felt like I could cry forever, the times I felt an emptiness, and ached for something I couldn't name. But I never completed the grieving because I denied I'd lost anything.

Gail taught me that I could redirect my energy to face, feel and express my sorrow. Grieving brought acceptance of losses so they could be left in the past. But just like recovering in other aspects, I had to face my losses and feel my sadness gradually at different stages. By giving up my grandmother's secrets and dealing with my family's reactions, I faced the truth of my life on a deeper level. Here I found the loss of the childhood I never had and the nurturing family I never would have. By mourning these losses, I freed myself to create a life I could enjoy.

* * * * *

JUNE 13

CHILDHOOD'S END

My grandmother told me
in *Gan Aeden*[1]
there is no death.
We snuggle in Daddy's chair,
watching Saturday Night at the Movies.
In the warm curve of her arm
I forget
that she is the biting snake.
My grandmother bakes blueberry pie,
feeds squirrels,
comes into my bed at night,
hurts me.

Though the world is calling me
I linger in the garden,
with all its dreads,
paradise still.

My grandmother lives
in *Gan Aeden*
waiting for my tears
to release
goodbye
with love.

JUNE 15

A dream from last night:
I was crying out "Mama, stop. Please don't, Mama." I felt as if
knives of pain were cutting outward through my skin. Once they were

---

1 the garden of Eden

out of my skin they were gone, but getting through! An old woman whom I knew and trusted had her hand on my back. She was telling me to let it out and I was trying. The old woman was tall and thin with white hair. She was strong and I loved her. The dream was very vivid.

I'm sad. The pain was so real. But cuts can heal and once it was out, it was gone.

JUNE 17

I'm sitting in the park. It's lovely here, cool and peaceful. I like watching the kids play.

JUNE 26

Well, well, well! I had a terrific time at Ilanna's party on Friday. I felt comfortable and had so much fun.

I've told Gail I can't talk to men as people and feel uncomfortable around them. I think there's some horseshit there because how come I had such a good time and had no problem talking to men at the party, until 4:00 a.m. actually. This is like the belief that I am shy, a family myth that is far from the truth. I have problems around my self image and my sexuality, which affect my interactions with men, but I am not shy around men any more than I'm shy around women.

JUNE 28

I'm full of an "isn't it good to be alive" excitement. I've been on the phone all afternoon. Ann keeps laughing affectionately, saying she can't believe the change. Three weeks ago it was "men? men who?" She says I sound sixteen, bubbly and confident. I'm thinking of asking out one of the men I met at Ilanna's party.

JULY 5

I dreamt I was standing outside. Eugene was there. He had long greasy hair and was staring at me. I asked him why, and he said because somebody killed Napoleon Bonaparte. I knew he meant I'd killed him. I said, "if you don't back off I'll show you who." He did and I drove away through slush. Cars were driving on the wrong side of the street. As I turned into my parents' driveway, it was spring and I was a kid parking my bicycle. My brother (not Ted) hugged me and I told him about Eugene. Then I blocked my ears and screamed at the top of my lungs. I woke up scared.

JULY 10

It's peculiar. Lately I've been full of zest for living, then sad and depressed, by turns.

JULY 16

THE LOSS OF CHILDHOOD
You devoured my childhood, Mama,
as if it came from the tree of life.

I lost ignorant bliss, safety, dependence, validation,
the pleasures of my body,
the mastering of a world my size,
the discovery of my powers,
trust, comfort, sharing, kindness,
belief in
my eyes and ears,
my worth, my heart,
the growing years.

In your greed you stole my childhood,
left behind
the burning emptiness of loss.
In your terrible hunger
you forgot that you loved me
forgot
you were my Mama
and I loved you.

JULY 19

For the first time, while I cried, I could really feel Gail patting my back. I felt it all the way inside and drew comfort from it. As well as pain and grief, I felt my love for her.

JULY 23

Went to a party yesterday on the spur of the moment. There weren't any men who interested me at first and then I spotted someone coming in. I thought he was cute. I looked at him and he looked at me. Then he came over and introduced himself. We got to talking and it was lots of fun.

JULY 26

Last night I dreamt I was writing a story. I wrote "She was raped. By her grandmother. Yes, you read that right. She was raped by her grandmother."

XVI

Rape

Words enabled me to survive, providing relief from abuse in reading and creating fantasies. My stories preserved my identity and sustained my sense of reality. Though I loved words, I rationed them, without being aware of it. Otherwise they might have revealed more reality than I could take. Living with my family, I wrote sporadically. In my marriage, I wrote nothing. In therapy, I unconsciously restricted my use of words while developing the skills and strength to handle what they revealed. Discussing subjects I really wanted to avoid, I often veered off into never-never land, using vague words that neither Gail nor I could make into sense.

In writing I connected with the inner me. I didn't know what I'd find inside myself or how it would feel to reclaim parts that were still hidden. My fear of the unknown made me waffle about writing. I told myself that I wasn't a poet, that I could write certain kinds of stories and not others. The affirmation I received in group and individual therapy gave me the security I needed to risk greater knowledge of myself. I began to write differently. I experimented with my writing and devoted more time to it, gradually losing my timidity. But in both writing and speaking I continued to use ambiguous words which hid the full extent of my wounds.

Whenever I refused to honour my strength and get on with recovery, my dreaming self gave me a shove in the right direction. This time, it jolted me with the word "rape," a word from which there was no hiding the extent of my hurt. The boundaries of my person had been smashed: the right to be safe, the right to own my body, the right to refuse, the right to feel, see, know and speak. Integral parts of my life had been ripped from me and possessed by my family and my husband: my body, my sexuality, my voice, my feelings, my work, my thoughts. I could never change the fact of my rape, or what I lost through being raped. But I could repair my boundaries in the present. I could reclaim ownership of myself. I could choose to let in just those people who would give me the respect and care I deserved.

Accepting the word "rape" opened up a whole class of words I had previously avoided because they were too explicit, too close to the bone. In dealing with my reaction to rape, I discovered I was strong enough to use these words, strong enough to bear the feelings they evoked and the reality they revealed. I no longer needed to ration or restrict my use of words. Writing with greater clarity and force, I could reach in to recover the deeper parts of myself. As I did so, those parts infused my recovery with the power they contained. I still got scared and at times lost sight of my purpose, retreating from the hard work of recovery. But with my dreams to give me a push and writing to reflect my inner vision, unclouded, my sense of purpose was restored. All the pieces of myself, broken and scattered by rape, were coming home to form a whole me.

*   *   *   *   *

JULY 26

RAPE

I turn to the dictionary for denial. Rape can't be what happened to me, that grim brutality. My dictionary says to rape is to violate, to violate is to transgress unjustifiably, to injure by violence, to break in upon, disturb, to interfere with rudely or roughly; to treat without proper respect or regard, doing injury in this way. My dictionary says that rape is the act of taking anything by force.

I was raped.

Easier words protected me from this depth of knowledge.

I was hurt. I was used. Hurt can be a smack on the butt.

But rape — rape screams the truth.

Rape screams that my grandmother beat me. There were times I thought I'd die. And when she was done, she'd toss me into the closet where hell stunned me with its cruelty, urging submission to the nauseating violation of my body.

Rape screams that my big brother whom I admired as grown-up and smart broke what was left of trust and shut me away from hope in the loneliness of abuse.

Rape screams that my husband tormented me with curses, threats, kicked-in walls, dinner thrown at the ceiling, and public humiliation that left me trembling, amenable to torture, beatings, the degradation of my sexuality under his command, running naked through the street, a blow job in the park, leash and collar, the endless submission to his fat belly crushing my arms, face, hips, holding my breath until he snored his satiety, and I silently cried.

Yes, I was raped. Repeatedly. That means over and over, roughly 4,000 times. Like a child, I count my fingers and toes and look up, bewildered at the enormity of this number.

I ask my dictionary to explain rape in the thousands, but it is mute, cold, dry.

JULY 29

Before I wrote "Rape," I saw my past as a series of still photos. My life looked blurry as if I weren't wearing my glasses. Now my past is like a film I can clearly see.

JULY 30

I'm turning over in my mind the definition of violate: "to treat without proper respect and regard, doing injury in this way."

I felt like a whore because I traded my body and soul to get Eugene to stay with me. But I wasn't standing on a street corner. We were husband and wife. I shouldn't have had to be abused to keep him from leaving. He had a choice — to stay or go. Instead, he raped me. I allowed myself to be raped because I didn't know any better, but I wasn't a whore. It's mind-boggling and I haven't totally accepted it, but I'm getting there.

AUGUST 5

I cried when I saw Gail today and feel much better for it. I still have to work at giving myself permission to cry, but it's so good to be able to. Sometimes I try to choreograph my feelings instead of letting them dance their dance.

AUGUST 8

By dressing in shapeless clothes, I not only avoid my sexuality, but also my connection to Mama as a woman.

AUGUST 9

I talked to Gail about her holiday today, or rather about how it reminded me of when Mum went to Israel. I cried as if my heart would break.

AUGUST 12

I bought a new lock for the door. I was surprised that it made me feel so much safer from Eugene. But now that I feel safe from outside danger, I'm left with what threatens me from inside myself. Before, the inside and outside were merged. My fears of what was inside me turned into fears of the outside. Since I've eliminated the outside threat, I'm left with facing all the things inside myself that still scare me.

AUGUST 14

I dreamt that Eugene and I were separating, but he threatened to kill himself. I was going back to Mum and Dad, though I would be leaving therapy before I was done, and leaving everything else behind. Then I realized that I didn't have to please Mum and Dad, I didn't have to go back after I separated.

This has been quite the week. After leaving Mum and Dad's old air conditioner sitting in my hallway for three months, I finally got it installed. Thank God! The heat melts my brains.

I'm contented with swirls of excitement — like chocolate swirl ice cream.

AUGUST 15

Happy Birthday! I'm pleasantly tired and mellow. Somehow I feel that everything's going to be okay. It's so good to be alive, really alive.

I look around and see my apartment and the cats, Mitzi on the coffee table, Snowball on the floor, and I feel blessed. What a contrast from two years ago! The cleanliness, the music, the tranquility, the caring people.

I'm going to be teaching advanced management accounting. Imagine that!

AUGUST 16

Mama in the kitchen with arm swinging
"I'll give you such a *zetz*[1] you'll go flying"
the crack of my head against the floor
"I'll give you something to cry for"
she hits and hits
so scared in the closet dark
rocking the hurt in my bones, I know what comes next
Mama please don't I want my mother
dead eyes peer into the closet
find me crouched in the corner
shivering sick on her bed if I throw up
she'll kill me I can't breathe she smells
my arm is going to fall off if I stop she will hurt me
so bad

"Ugly *farshtinkine moid*"[2]
kicking and screaming pulling my wrist gripped tight in
her fist
I am not ugly Mummy does so love me
You smell, not me not me
please not me

---

1 wallop
2 stinking girl

the black and red place swallows me
"her lips were red as blood"
I am so hot I wish I was dead

I like to kneel on my bed and look out the window
at three trees, they're little like me
I pretend they're big, they're watch guards
touching the sky
and I'm outside
the trees love me their branches are arms
hugging the empty place
I tell my doll stories she loves me
I wake up at the touch of a shadow
Mama at my bed and I fly into my stories
I always have to pee and it hurts between my legs
"Just lie with your legs apart and go to sleep"
I scream awake from nightmares
I'm too scared to open my eyes what if it isn't
a dream
I know the trees don't love me
my doll is just a doll
nothing matters anyway

AUGUST 18

Dad called to ask whether I'd come to a family session with the psychologist they'd seen at home. I found out from Dad that:

— he believed me at first but after he came home and thought about it he didn't;

— he hopes that through therapy I'll realize Mama didn't abuse me, and I'll find out the real reason for my problems;

— he told Mum and Ellen and Ted everything I said about Mama;

— they saw the psychologist just a couple of times and weren't in counselling; the purpose of this session was for them to air their feelings about my saying that Mama had abused me (that was the furthest thing from my mind, I had no idea that anyone else in the family had been told).

— it wasn't as horrible to think that something bad had happened to me as it was horrible to think that Mama had done something bad.

It hurts. I feel like there's a hole in my heart. I told Dad how much it hurt me. I'd felt so loved and supported by him and that's gone. I feel like an orphan. I have no family. I can't believe the thoughtlessness and cruelty of their asking me to come to their home ground so that the four of them could attack me. To what purpose? I thought Mum and Dad were in counselling and that I'd be returning their favour by coming to a session. But they're not in counselling. They're not working on this issue. They just want to bash me up. How could they? I empathized with the difficulties they have had in hearing what I had to say. I empathized with their pain. I expressed appreciation for Dad's support when he came to see Gail. I even expressed my appreciation for his allowing me to tell him how I felt last night. And I meant it. But they have shown no consideration of my feelings at all.

It hurts to realize that they really and truly believe I'm the crazy, the sicko. Somehow I thought maybe that was "just" my perception. Not even aware of it, I was still holding on to the myth that they did value me and I was unable to absorb it. You know, like there was a chemical missing in me that made me unable to take in their love. But now the truth is unmistakably plain. They value their illusions more than me and will readily sacrifice me just like when I was a child.

As difficult as this has been, I feel relieved. It's as if a weight has been lifted from me: the weight of hope and illusion and needing to protect my family. I can use my anger as fuel for action.

For some time I thought that eventually I wanted to speak publicly about recovering from abuse. Eventually has become now. The only way to stop abuse of any kind is to bring it into the open, so we can realize we deserve better. So we learn to identify abuse. So we know that no matter what the abuser says, abusive behaviour is not acceptable, and now that we are adults, we don't have to take it.

XVII

A New Heart

As children abused by our families, we were too young and weak to fend for ourselves. We did the best we could with what we had, surviving until, as adults, we could provide ourselves with the parenting we needed to finish growing up. We can be guided in this work by knowledgeable professionals, can read about it, watch films, attend lectures, model ourselves after mature people. But in the end, we do it ourselves. Slowly, at our own pace, in our own way, we grow ourselves up.

As far as I can see, the process of growing up is difficult and demanding for everyone. But for those of us who have been abused, there are some extra hurdles. In crossing these hurdles, we develop abilities which can foster our progress life-long.

In maturing we learn balance, which can enable us to live full, rational lives. Balancing risk and safety lets us try new things while maintaining sufficient stability to keep us grounded. Balancing work and play allows us to achieve and renew ourselves. A balancing of our own needs and the needs of our friends, lovers, families, coworkers, employees and bosses builds productive relationships. Utilising introspection and activity, body and mind in consort, involves us with both our inner and outer worlds. We begin to see ourselves realistically, to value our strengths, to forgive our faults and accept that we can try better next time.

In therapy I began to learn about balance when I saw myself teetering on the edge of a breakdown. I liked my extremeness. I saw it as alive and distinctive, but it wasn't worth falling apart for. I began by learning to balance work and play. When I discovered that a rest didn't make me a lazy pig, and that endless toil didn't entitle me to sainthood, I realized that things weren't always a matter of either-or.

It was possible that I was industrious about some things and lazy about others. I discovered that these characteristics couldn't always be categorized as either good or bad. Industry wasn't a good thing when it endangered my health. Laziness wasn't a bad thing when I was replenished by rest. I got to know how these traits of mine changed with circumstances: I was more industrious when I felt energetic, lazier when I was tired. The idea of degree began slowly to sink into my brain. Moderation came easier as I discovered that I was spirited and distinctive by being me, rather than by being extreme. The more I enjoyed my life, the less I needed intensity and extremeness to feel alive.

Learning to moderate my extremes was a gradual process. Gail pointed out where they caused me harm, leading me to inappropriate behaviour. In some circumstances I overreacted, straining my relationships. For example, Ann still comments on the time she was teaching me to sew and I practically ripped the sewing out of her hands because she was ordering me around. Other times I underreacted. I had no sense of proportion. I gave the same seriousness and intensity to where I shopped as I did to opposing racism. I didn't choose my battles. I fought everywhere or collapsed.

Gail showed me the range between all or nothing. Over the first two years of therapy, I discovered that instead of giving all, I could set limits without losing those who respected me. Instead of refusing to budge an inch from my ideas, I could give a little without losing myself. Being more tolerant relaxed my relationships. Teaching me to sew again, Ann expressed amazement at my patience and goodwill. I developed a greater awareness of what wasn't important to me and what was. Applying moderation gave me space to express my strong enthusiasms and beliefs. I chose where to put my intensity and where to fight my battles.

At the time I started therapy, I saw myself as made up of good and bad parts engaged in a fight-to-the-death struggle. Gail didn't view me as composed of "good" and "bad" parts. She saw me with strengths and weaknesses which were beneficial or detrimental to me, depending on the circumstances. I learned from her to work with myself, bolstering my strengths and minimizing my weaknesses, rather than persecuting myself with condemnation.

Making peace with myself took time and practise. It occurred as I reconnected my hidden parts, reclaimed my reality and detached myself from my family and Eugene. I was discovering that there was an alternative to collapsing my boundaries or fighting to the death: coexistence. Coexistence could allow me to live with the different aspects of myself in harmony. It could allow me to live peaceably alongside people who weren't just like me, nor I like them. It was permissible for me to be a unique, separate individual. I did not have to be enmeshed with anybody. Nor was I doomed to antagonism if I were not. I was allowed to grow up and live compatibly with other people.

Recognizing compatibility was a skill I developed. I picked it up partly through trial and error, and partly through getting to know myself. I noticed the kinds of people who brought out the best in me, and those who played on my weaknesses. As I became more aware of my views, I was attracted to people who shared or accepted them. I realized that people who were hostile to my priorities didn't fit well into my life. Those who respected me and had some common interests were congenial. The crux of my dilemma lay in accepting that my family and I were not compatible. To grow up and take charge of my corner of the world, I had to find a way to live without their blessing.

It was especially difficult for me to acknowledge that my father's views were inimical to mine. The family saw us as two of a kind, the silent pair. Our special bond had been a lifeline for me in my childhood, giving me a certainty of love and value. My father and I shared interests, sympathy and silence. But I was no longer willing to pay the price for silence. I spoke out, breaking our tacit agreement to play along with the family lies. My father could not take this threat to his tranquility. He chose to deny my reality instead. Leaving the silence meant that I had to leave my father behind, though I carried with me the gifts of love he gave me. It was a hard task. I cherished our old bond and the new bond between us was not yet forged. But it was made a little easier by the realization that I was not only being left through his denial. I was choosing to leave him, and the rest of my family, with their beliefs and their script, to find a place where I could be myself.

* * * * *

AUGUST 19

I just had the weirdest dream: I was on the phone talking to Gail, so I thought, but the voice was older, deeper, hoarser. The person on the other end of the line was very warm and comforting, supportive and honest. Then I realized it was my subconscious. I was aware that I was sleeping. She said she wanted to talk more but there was a beep on the line. I told her I'd hold. She said she couldn't do that because the other person would hear the beeps. I said, "No wait. Don't go. There can't be anyone there. You're *my* subconscious."

She answered, "I'm really sorry, honey. But I have to go." Then I was in the car with Dad. I realized I had to leave him to talk to my subconscious. I had to leave him behind and he knew it. So I left the car and I was back on the couch, calling my subconscious on the telephone. I cried and cried. Then I woke up feeling good. When I was asleep, I knew I was crying for what I've lost, the hopes and illusions I've had to let go because of finding out that Dad doesn't believe me.

AUGUST 21

Last night I was excited about starting a new notebook. But this morning, as I transfer papers from the old one, I feel sad. I'm leaving something of my past behind in that last notebook and it's hard to let it go.

SEPTEMBER 1

Mum and Dad want me to see the psychologist they've spoken with. I called her at their request. I found her slippery — full of rhetoric and difficult to pin down. The gist of what I got out of our conversation is that she believes she can judge, on seeing me, whether I was, in fact, abused by my grandmother. She thinks that if she decides I was not abused, she can then convince me of that. Her objective is to get the whole family to share the same perspective. She believes we could come to some kind of consensus after one or two or several sessions.

She said, "The objective in these situations is to repair the family relationships. It's a family issue and the family has to be helped with what's best for the family."

I answered, "No, the objective is for me to help myself get on with my life and for each person to do the same. I'm responsible for myself and they're responsible for themselves."

To which she said, "There's nothing more to discuss, then." I felt guilty because she told me earlier that she couldn't help Mum and Dad without seeing me, so I started backpedalling. Though I have no intention of seeing her, I felt intimidated and responsible for my parents. I felt like an uncaring person for my unwillingness to help them by meeting this psychologist. So I said I would think about it at some later time.

I'm mad. I feel emotionally hostaged. Why do we all have to share the same perspective? Let them live with their views. I have to. By making me responsible for my family's well-being, that psychologist is reinforcing the destructive relationships in my past. I've worked hard to detach myself from people who made me the target for what was wrong in their lives, who made me responsible for healing them. I feel hounded by her and by Mum and Dad. I'm struggling to maintain my equilibrium.

If being crazy means that I can write, that I can speak out to help other incest survivors, prevent abuse or raise awareness; if being crazy means I can live my life the way I choose, able to relate to people, open and comfortable in my skin, then it's a good thing to be crazy.

SEPTEMBER 8

Mum and Dad asked me whether I spoke to the psychologist. I told them I had, but as far as I could see, we would not be able to reach a consensus. I said that before I decided to tell them about Mama, I searched myself inside out to be absolutely certain of what I knew. Nothing they or anyone else could say would convince me that I was not abused by Mama. I asked them if anyone could change their view. Mum answered that she would never believe it. I said we have to live with the way things are. Their reactions to that:

Mum: "I'm sorry we can't be a family. You can't visit on the holidays. We can't share things. There are bad feelings. I hoped therapy would help you."

Dad: "It is incomprehensible how it could happen under my own roof. If I believe you, my world is shattered."

I've been so sad and depressed by turns. I keep thinking I should do something to help myself out of the doldrums, but I feel too lethargic. Underneath the depression is hurt, loss, and sadness.

SEPTEMBER 10

Dad taught me that on Rosh Hashana, the world is created anew out of chaos. The leaves turn, like fire dancing, and everything begins again.

SEPTEMBER 14

I have a picture in my mind. I am inside the hole in my heart, watching Dad recede, getting smaller and smaller, looking older and weaker. It makes me so sad. Then I see myself with my back to Dad. I must go in the opposite direction, growing with wings of colour as I emerge into a new place.

SEPTEMBER 15

Going through my financial records to calculate my tax estimate, I saw how much less money I earned this year compared to last. My priority last year was paying off my debts, which I did. This year my priorities have been therapy and writing. I returned to group, spent less time on chargeable work and more time writing. Last year I was successful by Mum and Dad's standards. This year my energy has gone into developing myself. I get upset about earning less money because it shows my separation from Mum and Dad, giving up their approval and honouring my own. It shows the importance I give to writing in my life. In reflecting my truth, writing opposes their version of reality. By acknowledging and living with its importance in my life, I enfold myself and give them up.

SEPTEMBER 16

I just woke up from a dream. I was saying, "I'm glad when boundaries are clear. If boundaries are confused, it's like when I was a child and there were no boundaries. It's very hard for me to impose boundaries on top of the confusion." I had a vivid mental image of a grey fog. I was trying to push down a circle of boundary with my hands, but the fog was thick and resistant.

SEPTEMBER 20

I've decided not to fast on Yom Kippur because when I fast I only think about being hungry. Instead, I've set aside the day to think. I don't need to atone. I've atoned too much in my life. We say that on Yom Kippur, God forgives everybody who repents by acknowledging their wrongs and turning to a better path. We're supposed to help people in this process of repentance by forgiving them. Well, I want to think about forgiving myself.

SEPTEMBER 21

YOM KIPPUR

All is forgiven,
dropped like a dead weight
the prosecuting angel has no power
to accuse me on this day.
I am the judge without compassion
condemn myself to carry
the heavy weight of wrongs
against myself,
wrongs I righted
long ago.

I hold my accusation to me
a suit of armour
blocks the penetration
of knowledge
encloses me,

immobilized,
concealing the shape
of memory, emotion, sex.

With my armour I am the judge.
Without my armour I am a woman
standing on a mountain,
fists against the sky
screaming with hate,
a woman
crouched in the pit,
rocking on her heels
in dismay
a woman
inside a body
that was hurt
and violated
and sickened.

This day is a solemn sabbath of rest.
It is my duty to forgive,
to shed my armour
and stand naked before God,
with scars and sores
so ugly it hurts to see,
to make me
a new heart
a new spirit
in my female body.

Dear God, what you ask of me is so hard.
Hear my prayer:
help me to forgive myself.

XVIII

Sh'ma

Two years prior to starting therapy, on the eve of Yom Kippur, the holiest day of the year, I got a phone call from my brother. "I would like your forgiveness for anything I might have done to offend you," he said.

Heart in my mouth, I answered, "I've distanced myself from you because of what happened between us when you were sixteen and I was ten." I explained that I didn't know how to deal with it and needed the distance until I could. He responded by asking again if I would forgive him for anything he might have done to offend me. I said, "okay." It wasn't that simple.

Forgiveness is about release: release from resentment and punishment, release from claims of obligation. That release is achieved with work. Judaism describes the work as a turn, a process of changing direction. It consists of taking responsibility for wrongdoing, acknowledging it to the one who has been harmed, if possible, and resolving to do right. Forgiveness is the recognition of that work. Ted never admitted his responsibility or the harm he did. How could I forgive him?

Yet I couldn't forgive myself for the misery I experienced in being abused, despite the work I did to better my life. I resented myself for being susceptible to harm, for having a body that could be injured and a soul that could be afflicted. I thought of forgiveness as a thing I had to find. But it was an evolution of examination, healing and creation. Through this evolution, a fragmented, terrified child, occupying an adult's body, was transformed into an independent, mature individual. It began with my decision to enter therapy. As I forgave myself a little,

I released some of my resentment toward myself and felt more peaceful. I liked myself better. I discovered that it wasn't my job to carry blame. I allowed myself greater freedom to feel and enjoy life.

By reclaiming and healing parts of me damaged by abuse, I released some of my shame and disconnection. Then I asked myself whether this was enough or if I would do more. Initially I made this decision unconsciously, but in my third year of therapy I became aware that I had a choice. I followed my own pace, forgiving myself as I was able to endure the pain of remembering abuse, to trust the process of healing and to accept its eventual outcome: growing up.

I was scared to grow up. I was good at certain grown-up things, like budgeting and taking charge at work, but I realized this wasn't the sum total of grown-up life. I wasn't ready to explore parts of me I associated with maturity: work, sexuality and community. I never sat down and said to myself, "Don't be sexual." But when I dipped my toes in these grown-up waters, feelings relating to abuse overtook my present-day experience. Avoiding those areas of my life enabled me to concentrate on dealing with my childhood, though it required me to suppress certain aspects of myself.

I handled my Jewishness by largely ignoring it. I rarely celebrated holidays or involved myself with the Jewish community. At holiday times I often felt too sad to celebrate. Waiting for the relief that came when the holiday was over, I coped by visiting friends who weren't Jewish. I cut myself off from tradition because it connected me with my abusers. Until I could accept that connection, tradition was too hurtful a reminder. On occasion I tried to participate in the Jewish community but I found it stressful. I felt I was accepted under false pretences, believing that any Jews who discovered I had been abused would repudiate me the way my family did. I resented the community for the myth that bad things didn't happen in Jewish families. The abuse in my family made me different, I thought. I didn't belong. It was painfully restrictive to be cut off from my heritage, my religion and my community. But the experience of my Jewishness overwhelmed me with family associations. I couldn't handle those associations while working to detach myself from my family. When I discovered my inherent worth, apart from them, I was able to renew my ties to Judaism.

Like my Jewishness, I avoided my sexuality. I seldom swam and never danced, though I loved to, because I felt physically and sexually alive when I exercised. My fear of sexuality was reflected in the way I dressed. As I grew to like myself, I began to wear pretty colours and soft textures, but my clothes had to be long and loose, hiding my shape. Going out with men was out of the question. Adult sexuality was too frightening. I was scared that something in me had caused sexual abuse or that my sexuality could cause me to be abusive. I was scared of the memories that might be aroused by experiencing my sexuality, scared of discovering unfamiliar positive feelings that would let me know just how awful sexual abuse really was. These fears stopped me from expressing my sexuality, from writing about it or even discussing it with Gail. My avoidance was wise. Dealing with the incest was scary enough without adding the fears of my adult sexuality. As I dealt with the incest by remembering and expressing my feelings about it, my fears lessened. I discovered that I didn't cause it and realized that my feelings were not overwhelming. I learned that I could handle memories. Gaining confidence in my strength, I prepared to face my sexuality.

I didn't avoid work since it paid the bills. But I avoided success. My parents thought little of what was most meaningful to me: writing and working for myself. As long as I yearned for their approval, I couldn't take my work seriously. Stifling my abilities made life simple. I went to therapy and group. I made a little money. I wrote. This simplicity allowed me to direct my attention to recovering from the abuse. As I progressed in therapy, my need for simplicity slowly diminished. I devoted more time to writing and began to submit it to magazines. I found more interesting work as a self-employed C.A. At the same time I continued to limit myself, not yet ready to completely detach my way of life from my family. However, by dealing with my wish for their approval and developing faith in my values, I laid the groundwork to define success in my own terms.

During my first two years in therapy, I reclaimed many aspects of myself. I learned to feel and express my feelings. I discovered my true nature, as distinct from my former family role, and came to enjoy healthy relationships. Though childhood memories and feelings still affected me, I'd recovered enough to begin exploring the parts of me that formed my mature identity. Like all the work of forgiveness, it was a gradual process and non-linear. The child I was, the young woman I'd been and the adult I was becoming were interconnected. Grown-up waters led back to unresolved childhood issues and forward to my marriage. Now I was strong enough to stay afloat in these waters, wherever they took me.

Integrating the adult parts of my life didn't begin with the bang I thought, but with a small change. Instead of treating sexual feelings as a distasteful intrusion, I began to tell myself they were healthy and positive, though I cried when I enjoyed feeling sexual.

Eugene had told me my sexuality was sick and dangerous, claiming to provide my sickness with an outlet so I wouldn't succumb to my real nature as a "whore." My disdainful attitude toward my sexual feelings was based on Eugene's lies. In giving up the lies, I faced the real extent of the abuse in my life. My marriage had replayed my childhood. Eugene's contempt and blame were my grandmother's and my brother's. His violation repeated theirs. As I began to deal with that knowledge, I felt terrible pain. Every memory of my marriage brought with it memories of my grandmother and brother. I struggled with the choice between pain and healing, voicing my dilemma in "Yom Kippur." I didn't realize that in wanting to forgive myself, expressing my fears and searching for the strength to overcome them, I was doing the work of forgiveness. I was preparing to remove my armour and embrace my naked self.

*   *   *   *   *

SEPTEMBER 27

The first spring I was in therapy I thought I was feeling a lot, and I was — compared to numbness. If my feelings at that time were like a sepia photograph, then my feelings now are a coloured holograph. I wonder how I'll look back at this time. There are still parts of my life that are very limited — physical, sexual, and social. Maybe a year from now I'll see myself today as an unfolded flower. That's nice. I still devote a lot of energy to dealing with and bearing the pain of the past. Just imagine what it'll be like to be free of that. It's beyond imagining!

SEPTEMBER 28

Well, group started last night — pant, pant, gasp. I was okay afterward, wound up, unable to sleep, but not in a turmoil of torment. I'm glad I could tell my story in greater detail than I've been able to before. Gail isn't there and I missed her, but I felt on a level with the therapists. They are experts in their areas and I in mine. They can help me but I know best what I need and what's right for me.

OCTOBER 2

A dream from last night: Ellen sat beside me while I held a book that belonged to the Guardian, looking at a page of pictures. I was to choose one of them. I saw a picture I liked but thought I should look at all of them first. Ellen said that after I made my choice, I would die. Then she was going to get my soul. I wasn't sure that my death was inevitable. The picture I liked was beautiful, full of colours, and "*Shehehianu*" was written on it. I thought if I chose that picture I wouldn't die. I wanted to ask the Guardian about it. I told Ellen and she said I had to die because she was expecting my soul. She'd already bought something on the basis that she would get my soul and the money that went with it. While we were talking the book closed. I opened it, looking for the page with the pictures, feeling alive and sexual. Then I woke up.

I asked Susan today what *Shehehianu* (a Hebrew word) means. She said, "who gives us life" — isn't that neat!!

OCTOBER 3

Eugene was a sadist; and I wasn't a masochist. I was lost and lonely and confused. I didn't know what I felt. I didn't know where the boundaries were. I didn't know what abuse was. I thought I was getting all that I deserved.

The essence of our relationship was that, under threat of separation, I was forced to do what I didn't want to, proving my devotion and worthiness through humiliation, pain and service. It makes me so mad and so sad. What a bastard!!

It's hard to feel that I lived with Eugene, abused by him.

OCTOBER 4

I had a lot of dreams about Eugene last night. I kept killing him but he wouldn't die.

I've noticed that I'm much more aware in group. My feelings flow freely and I express them more easily.

OCTOBER 6

I finally got the nerve to ask Ann if she thinks I'm fat and ugly. She said definitely not, far from it. I feel so warmed by her answer. She seemed surprised by the question.

I've been thinking about this fat and ugly business, and the issue of my sexuality. It seems to me that fat means undesirable and ugly means undeserving. Fat is the protection, the numbness, the thought that it wasn't me who was abused. It is distance. Ugly contains my sense of blame, of being garbage.

As I was thinking about "ugly," it came to me that somehow I thought I caused Mama to abuse me after we moved. In the old house I recognized that I was the target, not the cause. I thought I must be bad to be chosen as the target, to be left unprotected, but I knew I didn't make Mama do it. What changed in the new house?

In the room we shared I used to go to Mama's bed when I had a bad dream. I felt comforted. I thought she came into my bed to get paid back. I asked for it. It makes me cry, remembering the child I was, believing I asked for abuse by asking for comfort. I was not to blame. It's like my marriage, thinking I had to pay to keep Eugene. Thinking I was a slut. No wonder it's been so hard in my adult life to ask for what I need.

OCTOBER 7

I got my divorce certificate today. HURRAY!!! Three cheers for me! YAY!

It's very timely too. I woke up this morning feeling wonderful, as if a weight had been lifted off me. I've been so scared of the horror locked in the closet. When I finally opened the door, all I found was a sad, little girl whom I took in my arms. I feel like dancing for joy.

OCTOBER 12

There's a woman in group who struck me as more needy than any of us. She takes up a lot of time, not working to solve her problems or deal with her feelings, but demanding attention and hand-holding. I resented it because we all need to work. She also scares me. She seems like a powder keg ready to go off. While someone else was working, she was kicking a pillow. With every kick, my stomach fell. I talked to her about it in group, trying to be as gentle and tactful as I could while being honest. I'm glad and proud that I could take care of myself.

OCTOBER 14

I feel as though I've been insubstantial, shimmery with vague outlines. I imposed on myself an exoskeleton that supported me. It enabled me to do many things but was also restrictive and inflexible. Gradually my exoskeleton has been dissolving as I've become more substantial from inside. That substance has allowed me to realize that I can trust myself to know what I need to write. I can trust myself to know that I will. It's this part of me, the solid part, and my faith in it, which was violated, raped and beaten.

Gail asked me what I want to do with my writing. The question scares me. The answer is really who I am as an adult.

OCTOBER 15

It hurts so much to feel the emptiness, to give up my dreams of childhood. But I don't belong in Paradise. It is the province of ghosts. To continue writing means I have to grow up, fill out into reality, sexuality. Though I cry savage tears, I am hungry to know the grown-up me, the writer of maturity.

OCTOBER 21

A letter, never sent:

Eugene:

The nicest thing I can say about you is that you're fat, you smoke, and you have a heart murmur. Maybe you'll relieve the world by kicking off.

You turned everything lovely into something ugly. You blamed me for it as if the ugliness came from inside me. But it didn't. The ugliness was inside you, a cesspool of crap that you tried to drown me in. I was young, scared and vulnerable. You used every bit of that to manipulate me, exhausting me with your threats and anger, putting all the responsibility on my shoulders.

You are mean, nasty and vicious. You are a bully and a coward. I wasn't a person to you. Just like with my grandmother and my brother, I was a thing, a soft thing to be abused.

I can't understand how you could treat me so badly. I did nothing to deserve it. I deserved to be treated decently, like a human being, but you treated me like garbage. You used me. You raped me. You beat me. You humiliated me. Even though you are less than nothing, I'm hurt that you could do that to me because once I thought I loved you and I turned myself inside out to please you. You were my husband and you betrayed me. You said you loved me but you acted as if you hated me.

OCTOBER 22

I'm a rotten judge of character, so how can I trust anyone? How can I believe any of the nice things people have said about me? How can I trust my own judgment? My world seems topsy-turvy, a familiar feeling.

On top of all that I accidentally drove over a curb and broke the exhaust pipe!

OCTOBER 25

Last night I dreamt that I was talking to Gail and I started to scream this high-pitched endless scream because I knew something had happened to me when I was twelve.

I remember worrying about being pregnant when I was twelve, thinking of the man who had molested me in the music school. I felt tormented by my fear, even though I knew he just made me poke him with my finger. When it happened, the year before, I didn't have my period yet, but I still worried.

OCTOBER 26

I had the most wonderful dream: Demons and spirits from hell appeared to take me over, but I kept talking about belief, how all you have to do is believe, that's all that is important. People began to join me. The more of us there were, the stronger we were and the more protected from the denizens of hell. By this time we were in a big hall. In hell they realized this was a real threat so they sent one of the top demons. She asked why we talk about belief, why don't we talk about reality, like stones and earth, like science? I said that stones and earth were real but reality can always be disproved. All science is based on first principles, which are assumptions. They can't be proven. You have to believe. It doesn't matter what or how or why you believe. The important thing is that you believe. I kept saying it over and over. All the people were saying the Sh'ma,[1] more spirits joining us all the time. I was walking hand in hand with Ellen, who was two years old. She was tired and so was I. My voice was hoarse. But I knew I had to keep going or the spirits would backslide, and the denizens of hell were waiting. I had to watch out for infiltrators who would pretend to believe but were trying to sabotage us. There were also denizens from hell who were trying to trap me by distracting me or making me doubt. Even though I was tired, I felt good. I knew this was right.

I woke up saying over and over that you have to believe and I knew it was a message about faith in myself. The denizens of hell

---

1 meaning, "hear," this is the first word of the most important Jewish prayer, which begins, "Hear, oh Israel, the Lord, our God, the Lord is one."

were the forces inside and outside me that try to undermine and make me doubt myself like I did on the weekend. The spirits saying the *Sh'ma* were the forces that are supportive. I have to work to keep those forces around me. I need to remember: all that matters is belief. That's the basic principle.

I feel good!

OCTOBER 30

What a night, talk about nightmares! In one of them I was a child, hiding somewhere, surrounded by adults. One old goat said to me, "Well, you wanted to be an adult. Come on, kiss me. Be an adult." I knew that wasn't the kind of adult I meant and I was terrified, screaming.

NOVEMBER 3

Listen to this! In group Anna told us about a conference for therapists on starting incest survivors' groups. She asked if anyone would be willing to talk about the process of therapy and the group experience. I had mixed feelings. Today I decided I'd call for more information.

At first that made me want to hide away. But then I thought of suggesting I read my poetry, something I have no doubts about wanting to do. I discussed it with the organizer, and she thought it was a great idea. I am so excited! Nervous too.

NOVEMBER 6

I've been dreaming about Ted. My head hurts. It's time for me to deal with my feelings about him again, and about Mum and Dad and their reaction. It seems so hard to go back to it. I thought I was at peace in my feelings toward Ted, but I'm not. I'm angry. I feel betrayed, both in relation to the past and the present. I'm angry about the abuse being buried by Mum and Dad. I don't want to feel this way. I want to be unaffected by it, but I'm not.

Sometimes I feel so frustrated by all that I still have to deal with.

I'm very excited about Friday. My first time reading in public! Last night I thought of applying for a Canada Council grant to write my book. But that seems so frighteningly real. So grown-up. My dreams may come true and I want to laugh and cry and hide.

NOVEMBER 7

I don't know whether my writing is good or important but I know it's what I have to do. I must think it could make a difference or I wouldn't have offered to read my poetry at the conference, would I? It would be a scary thing to acknowledge that I have been given a gift. What I do with it is my responsibility, defining what I'm going to be when I grow up.

NOVEMBER 8

I feel as though I've been in the middle of a river for the last couple of years. I make just enough money to fill my basic wants. I work on therapy and group. I write. But it's all very much in the present, without past or future. Now I'm trying very hard to stay in one place because I'm coming toward a place where the river branches. I was talking to Alma about it yesterday, around midnight. Alma is a down-to-earth person, not usually fanciful. There must have been something in the air last night. She was looking at the light bulb inside her lamp, she said, and saw that one of the river branches had trees along it in beautiful autumn colours. That's where I should go. I asked, "Is that where I get a grant?"

Alma looked into her light bulb and said, "Yes. But along that branch are rapids."

I asked her what the rapids were, and she said "success."

Yes, and ouch! I'm scared! I want to run away, cry, hide in bed.

NOVEMBER 9

My moods have been so volatile the last couple of days. I don't know what's going on. I was anxious all day yesterday, and in a fret. I thought, "I don't want to grow up. I don't want to end group or therapy. I want to quit. I don't want to be direct. I want to be indirect. I don't want to be positive. I want to be a slob." It got so wild, I started to laugh. Another one of my frets was, "It starts with reading poetry. Then next thing you know one of my submissions will get accepted.

Then I'll get a grant and write a book. Then I might start to make money and be successful. No way, I'm not having any of that. I'm not!"

I've been bouncing around from one emotion to another — calm, excited, depressed, industrious, bored, scared. I'm flushed and have a headache. No wonder, I've felt enough feelings to last a month. And get this — after all that fear and no way, I found myself calling for information and grant applications. I don't know what's going on with me these days. I really don't. I feel like my head is overstuffed.

NOVEMBER 11

I'm sad and scared and tired. The poetry reading was different from what I expected. I thought I'd be numb or have no difficulty with it. In fact I felt what I read and it was difficult. Many nice things were said to me, though I found it hard to take them in. That disappoints me. Still, the reading has reinforced my desire to speak out on abuse in the way that I can. I want to do more.

NOVEMBER 13

I had the neatest dream while I was napping: I was doing some kind of study and I wanted to give a questionnaire to a math class. It was adapted from a book called Limits of Mathematics. The professor said he disagreed that there were limits. I started to say I'd just adapted the questionnaire and I didn't believe in limits either. In fact, I've had flashes of understanding infinite dimensions. He interrupted me and said I could give the questionnaire in twelve minutes. I ran to another building to make copies. I thought about telling him that I not only have the creative, intuitive side of me, which gives me the flashes of understanding, I also have the other side to do something with it, the side with staying power that got me my C.A. As the dream ended, and before I woke, a voice said, "You can choose the limits of despair or the limitlessness of hope."

That says it all, doesn't it? The limits are the limits I place on myself, flattening my own development. I can choose to keep those limits or let go of them and allow myself to grow freely. I like the way the dream showed me the value and necessity of both sides of me, the interplay between them. For so long I've kept them apart and put them down: the C.A. is stodgy, the writer is a dilettante. But each needs the other, the visionary and the businesswoman. Left hand and right coming together in another sense.

I'm excited and scared. Where am I headed?

XIX

A Flame of All Colours

My dictionary describes succeeding as accomplishing one's purpose, thriving, growing. Alma's vision in the light bulb was quite right. I was heading into success. My journey took me away from my family's definitions and toward knowledge of my own goals and direction. The autumn trees represented a time of change, giving rise to the potential of a new year. It was my hope for this potential that kept me going when therapy was rough.

My recovery proceeded unevenly. Sometimes I wanted to tear out my hair in frustration over my slowness, sometimes feelings and revelations tumbled over each other in a rush. During the periods of fast growth, I could hardly catch my breath. They were the rapids: scary, painful and exciting. Discovering my father's disbelief began one of these periods. It was an autumn of turbulence: vivid memories, forceful feelings, shifting perspectives and new knowledge. I was sure that I was on the verge of ending group and ending therapy couldn't be far behind. I was mistaken about ending group but I was right in sensing great change, out of which my purpose and direction were emerging. My course was taking me to a place where I belonged, a corner of the world I could call my own.

As a child, I believed I had no place in the world because it was less painful than recognizing that physical abuse, incest and denunciation were "my place." With Eugene I found much the same, exchanging incest for sexual abuse by my husband. Eugene and my family taught me that the problem was my unhappiness, not my situation. Gail introduced a novel idea. Rather than squish myself into a position that didn't fit my needs or character, I could find a place that was right for me.

The place I looked for was both physical and emotional, consisting of my environment, the people in it and my state of mind. My search began in therapy, with discovering alternatives to my childhood and marriage. I learned about safety and acceptance. I became aware of which surroundings, activities and relationships disturbed me and which I found satisfying. I began to put this knowledge into practice. I painted my apartment, walked in the woods, made and lost friends. But I directed most of my energy to discovering rather than to creating what I wanted. I drifted in the river, catching what floated close by, because I needed my energy for healing.

Drifting became familiar. Rowing under my own power, instead of following the current, meant choosing where I wanted to go. It required me to deal with the consequences of my choices. Any sort of change was a risk, and therefore scary. I was reluctant to venture into the unknown even though I had gained the strength to do so. As I faced the repercussions of my father's disbelief, however, I found myself taking up the oars. Though my conscious mind said, "I won't," the wiser part of me, which knew I was ready, pushed me to action. I started the grant application. I read my work in public. I dealt with my marriage and the memories of childhood abuse it aroused, releasing more energy for action. I rode the rapids with exhilaration, fear and a desire to get off the boat.

When my fears threatened to take over, my dreams mobilized me. They laid out my choices in dramatic language — life against death, spirits against demons, hope versus despair — renewing my determination to choose well. I wasn't fully aware of the significance of these dreams but they made me feel good when I was having a tough time. They put me in touch with the core of me, my connection with the infinite, stretching from the beginning of time to the unending future. This developing awareness of my spirituality buoyed me up when I was scared. Feeling a part of something bigger than myself deepened my sense of connection with the world around me. I grew more sensitive to what I had, what I lacked and what I wanted. While feeling the gaps more acutely, I also began to take in the affection of the people in my life. I became increasingly certain that my inner self was guiding me in the right direction, toward a place where I could live an active, full life in harmony with my core sense of connection. By risking change, by feeling my feelings, by facing my memories, I moved toward that place. Although I didn't know what success meant, I was achieving it.

*   *   *   *   *

NOVEMBER 14

I've been remembering more about Ted abusing me when I was twelve. His hand over my mouth as he pushes aside my blankets. I'm having trouble accepting it. When I do, I feel relieved. Then I go into another bout of nausea and memory. I have a sense of badness, some connection with Eugene and feeling like a whore. Then I doubt myself and feel depressed. When I talk about Ted I get so nauseous, I feel like my guts are turning over.

I've been dreaming about looking for a secret.

NOVEMBER 15

MY BROTHER'S SECRET
My brother owned a secret:
the reason for the moisture on his prick,
why he played odds and evens
with my body.
I asked him time and again
to reveal the secret meaning,
he turned his face from me.

My parents own a secret.
This little business of incest,
we talked with your brother
well, it's a matter of perspective,
you weren't abused.
Your brother is religious, has a wife,
three children, is a doctor.

What am I?

The possessor of fractured memories
pictures without sensation,
feelings without incident.
I remember touching and being touched
dread, curiosity, nausea, vomit, arousal,
and recognize the secret I wear like a second skin.

The secret is
my brother shakes with zeal at prayers
as once he shook abusing me;
my brother's smug piety once promised fun
while I smiled uncertainly at his bare skin
white as death engulfing me
until I found myself kneeling at the toilet
wondering at the strangeness of the colours in my vomit.

The secret is
my brother tucked me into his bed with a book of
    legends
when I scared myself reading *Jane Eyre*
no child at eleven
staring at his back while he studied,
signaled his desire with one, two fingers,
the odds/evens game to choose who's it,
always it, cold, scared,
glad to be chosen, wishing I weren't
because it makes me sick
but it's something I share with my brother.

The secret is
my brother was good, grown-up, smart.
What was I with this churning inside.
What was I when unpleasant tickles
turned to pleasure turned to pain

when I found myself
throwing up memory, head spinning
dizzy when I lay in bed —
dizzy feels better.
My brother makes me choose,
will I touch him first will he touch me.
I love my brother
he is good.
In dizzy confusion between horrors.
I ask "why am I me?"
he answers,
"you are a speck of dust in the universe."

The secret is
he is wrong.
I am an incest survivor
survived betrayal
survived violation
survived demotion
from female child to speck of dust.

The secret is
my brother, whom I loved so much,
raped me with assorted parts of his anatomy,
and abandoned me.
He *davens*[1] in a *shtibl.*[2]
My father reveres his piety.
My mother honours his position.
And I
sicken with the memory
of his shaking at his prayers
so much like his shaking against my skin.
I ache

---

1   prays
2   small group of very religious men who pray together

with the betrayal of my love
touch the lies that paint my skin ugly,
raw wounds beneath.

NOVEMBER 17

Whether or not there was intercourse when Ted abused me (and I'm still not sure), I was violated by him. The emphasis Mum and Dad place on intercourse makes me very angry.

NOVEMBER 18

When I look in the mirror I see a friendly face. I used to hate seeing my face in the mirror. It reminded me of Mama. Now I see someone who reminds me of Ann.

I got the information from Canada Council today. Much excitement and terror. Whether or not I get the grant, applying is a statement of my belief in the value of my writing. If I get the grant, as Ann says, then I'll have to write and not go around picking my nose, thinking about it. She sure has a way of putting things, doesn't she?

NOVEMBER 19

I've reorganized my filing cabinet. I took writing out of my "personal" drawer and moved it into one of the business drawers. It's a step in bringing my C.A. and writer parts together. I wrote a letter to the Explorations Program requesting a grant application, and one to an old professor, asking for a reference. This is my C.A. side saying "DO IT" while parts of me cower in fear. Well, "DO IT" has landed me in trouble, but it's also awfully handy in getting things done.

NOVEMBER 20

I want to stop liking or hating different parts of me because Mum and Dad would or wouldn't approve. They're unable to know or accept me. I have to find my own approval and my own definition of a grown-up me just as I've been discovering and growing to like myself all through therapy.

NOVEMBER 25

I feel discouraged and frustrated. What's the point of anything? Why shouldn't I just quit?

NOVEMBER 29

I worked in group on leaving my family. It hurt.

Anna had me sit in one chair and be the part of me that holds back, that is afraid the pain will kill me. In the other chair I spoke as the part of me that pushes forward. I've never heard it speak so distinctly. I saw it as the old woman in my dreams, an older, wiser part of me. I was surprised at what I said and felt sitting in that chair. At first I was sad, as if I had already felt this pain. Even so, I knew I had to go on or the growing part of me would die. Then I got angry and said that if I stopped here, I would be throwing away all that I've been given and I, the old woman, would not speak any more.

That scared me. I believe that if I deny myself, my unconscious will stop speaking to me in my dreams, through my body, in my writing, and I will lose my most powerful ally.

Anna helped me rejoin the parts of me, but what was strange is that I felt not unreal, but in another place. It was the place I am in when I write, a deeper place. I asked Anna for a hug and I felt the hug differently, deeper.

I picture the old woman walking with me, hand on my back, giving me her strength and love. She says I will not die of the pain. I ache for the world I've lost. I want it back. She promises a new world. She says I have to choose between my family and myself.

I stand inside myself and look back at Mum gathering light, blessing *Shabbas* candles. In two days it is Hanukkah. Dad sings *Maoz Tzur*, Rock of Ages. They sit around the table with Ellen and Ted and the children, eating *latkes*, playing *dreidl*. I am here, on my own.

Somehow I will find a way to celebrate without them.

DECEMBER 2

Gail says I keep a cap on myself in group. She thinks it's important for me to continue showing the deeper aspects of myself there, like the chair work I did, talking about my dreams, reading my poetry. It will lead to greater congruence because it counteracts the command of incest families to keep ourselves hidden and secret.

DECEMBER 5

Mitzi is fascinated by the Hanukkah candles. They're so beautiful, casting shadows on the wall that look like tall towers. Reading about Hanukkah, I found out that some people imagine God as a flame of all colours. We are the candle.

DECEMBER 6

I realize again that at the core of me is the great song of life, something infinite made small enough to fit inside me. I have an image of a diamond, all the faces being all the different aspects of me. A light shines from the centre through all the faces. It is the great song of life.

Talking about the image in group, I was surprised at my anxiety. I was scared because Mum and Dad would not accept the reality of my world, the world of the great song of life. They would call it a fantasy world, or crazy or silly. But if you take everything else away, that's what would be left in me. It is the wellspring of all that I am.

The group's response was appreciative and understanding. I couldn't take it in at first. When I woke up this morning I felt sad. But now I feel warm inside, and a bit amazed. I still don't quite get what they saw in me, but I'm glad they did. I like it.

DECEMBER 8

Dear God, thank you for bringing me to this place. The pain gets more intense and more difficult as I've grown, but my happiness and peace have also grown bigger. Big enough to fill a world.

DECEMBER 10

I had the most wonderful sleep this afternoon and the most incredible dream.

I dreamt that I was napping and I woke up laughing. Anna was waiting for me to wake up. As I did, she said she was glad I wasn't going to quit. She'd been waiting to find out. I threw off my old painted shower cap. It was the cap that Gail talked about. I said I didn't know why I always wore that when I was asleep. Then Anna said something about her role in my life because I was surprised that she was there, waiting for me to wake up. She came over to the armchair where I'd been napping and hugged me. We were rocking, hugging, until I woke up. The dream was amazingly vivid. The hug felt so deeply comforting, I wasn't sure whether I was dreaming or not. Even after the dream ended, instead of waking up or losing the feeling, I sank into a deeper sleep of total warmth and comfort. It was wonderful.

DECEMBER 11

I'm looking out the window at the evergreens. Snowball is asleep on his back, curled into a depression in the quilt. I'm happy.

DECEMBER 12

I woke up cranky today. Janet gave me a lovely Christmas card with an absolutely beautiful note inside that talked about how I've affected her. It touched me to the core because she isn't a gushy person. It overwhelms me. It hurts because in accepting her note, I am rejecting Mum and Dad's view of me. I hurt because they don't see me as she does. In recognizing that her note makes me feel successful in my life, I have to let go of Mum and Dad's definition of success, and of being successful in their eyes. I am so angry today. At Mum and Dad for putting me in the position of having to choose between myself and them. At all the people who've been supportive and responsive to me because that makes me see more clearly who I am. What I am is good, according to my system, which brings me back to giving up hope for Mum and Dad's approval. It hurts. This is hard.

DECEMBER 15

Before I fell asleep, I asked for a dream that would help me feel better or at least understand what's going on inside me. I was thinking about the story of Christmas and what it means. "Christmas is a promise of love," I thought, and fell asleep. In my dream, I heard "And voice after voice shouts, 'Glad tidings. Christmas is come.'"

DECEMBER 17

The issue is not only accepting Mum and Dad's limitations, but also taking the risk of allowing in other people who don't have those limitations, letting them into the deep part of me that was hurt and rejected. Revealing the deeper part of me and being hurt is familiar. Being appreciated is unfamiliar. If I take it in, I am vulnerable to betrayal. That's what is so hard.

I am crying because I feel all the good things that people have been saying to me, and it is beautiful.

1989

JANUARY 6

I feel full of fresh air and tingling in my legs. Janet and I went skating before midnight in the little rink across from her building. I was a bit scared and tottery to start, but I got into the swing of it quickly. So peaceful. And the motion. Afterward I sat for a few minutes, watching the trees, revelling in the quiet.

JANUARY 8

This break while Gail's on holiday is just what I wanted: a time to pause, take stock and clear my head. I made concrete plans for 1989, which I haven't been able to do before. I enjoyed Christmas with friends. I went to the museum, saw movies, swam, skated, shopped till I dropped. I cleaned out my closets and they're beautiful. I miss Gail, but I don't feel the sense of loss and abandonment I used to. I've had so much fun that I'm not keen on returning to therapy and inside stuff. But it's time to get back to business.

XX

The Sea of Strange

Life was pretty good. I felt happy and had friends. I was pleased with the direction my work was taking. I wondered, why go back to therapy? The summer before, I forayed briefly into the sexual universe. I went to a couple of parties, discovering to my surprise that I was relaxed and enjoyed myself. I even asked someone out and had a good time. But I wasn't ready to socialize with men. I didn't know why. I just felt something inside me loudly and firmly say no. Early in the new year, thinking it was time to challenge my fears, I tried forcing myself to socialize in mixed company. I couldn't do it. I realized then that feelings and memories which I hadn't fully confronted stopped me from relating to men, except in the most formal, professional situations. I could choose to stop therapy where I was, but it meant living out my life in an asexual world. To recover my sexuality, I needed to face and heal, on a deeper level, the damage caused by the sexual abuse in my life.

Sexuality is a part of our identity, formed by physical and emotional characteristics. It involves the way we express our identity and how we choose to enjoy it. Sexual abuse is not defined by enjoyment, but by the destruction of our choice. Sexual abuse is the rape of our very being. Our inner self is assaulted, we are violated physically by unwanted touch and emotionally by betrayal. The loss of our power to choose can lead us to be asexual or to offer our bodies indiscriminately. Sexual abuse teaches us shame, distrust and helplessness. When sexual abuse is incest, the violation is intensified by the knowledge that we are abused by those closest to us. The ones we love, those on whom our lives depend, rape our souls and allow us to be raped. There is no part of us that is sacred, that belongs to ourselves. We are offerings in the family volcano.

Sexual abuse is a trauma that involves every aspect of ourselves. We who survive develop powerful defense mechanisms. We commonly endure by leaving the scene and feeling as though we're somewhere else. We may be present but have a sense of unreality. We may split off the part of us that experienced it or numb ourselves physically or emotionally to blunt the impact. Dividing body and mind blocks memories from our consciousness. We can forget completely, recall only selected incidents, remember visually without emotions or physical sensation, remember feelings without visual recall of what happened. Because our memories are fragmented, it is easy to minimize them or feel crazy. Feeling crazy may be more bearable than believing the truth. By removing ourselves from the trauma, whether we deny it happened or dull our senses, we survive. The price we pay for survival is that we are out of touch with ourselves and our reality. Our abusers still own us.

I survived the incest in foggy oblivion. When my grandmother started to abuse me, I was too young to look for external hiding places. Instead I tried to be unnoticed. I learned to push down my feelings, to withdraw quietly into myself. As I got bigger, I hid at the neighbours, in our basement, outdoors. When she found me, I hid inside myself. In the new house I was unable to handle knowing I shared a room with the person who tormented me, so I completely forgot it. Family photographs show my grandmother's presence on occasions when I simply don't remember her being there.

Initially, while Ted abused me, I felt like a detached scientist taking note of curious details, without any emotion or physical sensation. Later, to survive his violence, I disconnected from my body, losing any sense of relationship to what "it" was feeling. I believed my body existed only to carry *me*, by which I meant my mind. Physically, I was almost numb. I retained fragments of his earlier abuse, which I remembered as a game between peers. When I found an old photograph of us at the time Ted was abusing me, I was shocked by the difference in our size: I was a little girl, he was a man.

The defense mechanisms that enabled me to survive the incest continued to operate in my marriage, removing me emotionally from trauma, blocking out signals that flashed, "this is destroying you, get out." But being an adult, even a squashed adult, I had alternatives I didn't have as a child. In the moment of torment I realized something was wrong and, when I could, I went for help.

Taking back ownership of myself meant repossessing my feelings and perceptions by giving up the defenses that blocked them. These defenses had saved my life. It was hard to let them go. Yet my numbness gradually receded and memories returned. I felt more real. My body and mind came closer together. I didn't advance at a steady pace in a straight line, sometimes my path rose to dizzy heights and sometimes it twisted back on itself, making me wonder if I'd actually got anywhere. Despite my uneven pace, I reached the stage where I was no longer numb, where I felt real and in possession of my memories, where I respected my body, paying attention to the messages it gave me. Coming into 1989 I felt pretty good about myself and my life. Yet, without articulating the ways I wasn't whole, I knew I wasn't ready to end therapy.

Though I respected and listened to it, my body was "it," an object, rather than me. My body and mind were like two eyes focusing separately. My feelings, memories and senses were blurred by this double vision, shielding me from the hideous view of incest and wife abuse. The time came for me to focus clearly. I had recovered myself to the point where I could face reality without my defenses to soften it. Tired out by the turbulence of the preceding fall, I proceeded inch by inch. As my mind and body drew together, I remembered my past with burning intensity.

Recovery is different for every person. Each of us has unique strengths and weaknesses as a result of our personality and history, whether we have survived incest, other forms of abuse or another trauma. Nevertheless we all choose to give up the defense mechanisms that protected us when we were weak, in favour of more effective ways of dealing with life. Tired, scared of painful feelings and new memories, I waffled at the edge of the fire, averting my eyes. I held myself back, avoiding poetry, keeping my dreams out of therapy. But in the end my desire to be whole mobilized me. I jumped into the fire.

* * * * *

JANUARY 11

Remembering the violation I experienced with Eugene, I feel as if someone is reaching into my chest and pulling my heart out by the roots.

JANUARY 14

I had the weirdest dream while I was napping: I was playing a game where you had to be a composer. I chose Beethoven. Gail asked me, in the dream, how I felt about being Beethoven. I didn't want to answer her, and I was crying inconsolably. Then I was Beethoven again, playing piano and humming what I wrote. There were people who wanted me to be put away and a lot who wanted me to be released. I was trying not to hear them shout, trying just to play. Then I woke up. Ever since, I keep hearing "The Song of Joy" in my head.

I wonder if it's the part of me that clings to the past that is being ripped out, like choking weeds pulled to make room for flowers and fruits in the hurt place opened to the sun.

JANUARY 17

I hate it when Gail brings up dating. The thought of it makes me want to scream and cry.

JANUARY 19

Starting this session of group was painful because I talked about my marriage for the first time there. I asked Janet if she thought I was a horrible person for living with Eugene. She said not at all. She hugged me and said I was loved.

I decided today that just because I'm depressed doesn't mean I have to starve, so I did some grocery shopping.

JANUARY 20

I can't wait to start another notebook. I want a new beginning, though I feel better after an evening at Janet's. I hate it when I get lost in despair: everything's bad, nothing matters, who cares. It makes me

feel ungrateful. I keep getting engulfed by gloom as if I were still with
Eugene. But I'm not. I have to forge ahead and remember why. I have
to keep counting my blessings. It was hard to go back to therapy and
group. It takes so much of my energy but it also gives me space and
energy for my real self, developing from the work I do.

JANUARY 21

EUGENE

Who is the woman that married you?
I don't remember me as her.
I was twenty
then thirty.

I am not the woman who lived with you,
but once I was.

You revelled in violation,
stroking my skin from toe to lips, erect
with pride: "I've used this and this and this,
I gave them all away. They're mine," you said.
My skin violated, muscles tense with bridled hate,
legs forced open to your touch, the touch of strangers
invading my body in shapes and smells and sweat
the memory of touch like hot glue
branding me hideous
raw
where you reached inside to rip.

I scream without end remembering
until
anger uncurls a hissing snake:
you won't destroy me, again.
I was your wife. I am no longer.
I walk back along the path through hell toward
that young woman, eager to be wife

to belong, beloved
lonely, waiting
for an invitation to belong again
to me.

JANUARY 27

On Wednesday I felt totally thrown back to my marriage and the person I am now was lost to me. I was anxious and scared and hurting beyond bearing. I went through my repertoire of things to make myself feel better, but nothing did. I called Gail. Hearing her voice steadied me and she assured me that this would pass.

I slept over at Janet's. She tucked me in and hugged me. She said I was safe, no one could get me. I felt warm and loved.

When I woke up I didn't feel like I was going to die. I was so relieved, I could dance on stars. The relief wore off but the pain was bearable. When I got home, there was a heartwarming message from Alma phoning to check how I was, and Ann said I should have called her too. It's nice to see my friends rally around me, to hear and feel their caring. Though it's hard, I feel as if I'm moving ahead, little by little leaving Eugene behind.

JANUARY 29

Yesterday was beautiful! I walked and shopped. I played hula-hoop, danced and went to a movie. I ticked off *15* items on my list of fun things, a new high.

FEBRUARY 2

I went swimming three times this week. I've been feeling so good and bad by turns, often at the same time.

FEBRUARY 3

Ted called Gail for an appointment! What the hell is going on? It's been over a year since I asked him to come for a session. I'll have to call him. I want to know his agenda before I agree to it.

FEBRUARY 10

I dreamt that I told Ellen how hurt I am that she won't talk to me.

FEBRUARY 12

I was depressed yesterday, feeling blobbish and lethargic, like I was wasting my life away. Doesn't that sound familiar? That's how I felt when I met Eugene. Last night I had wonderful flying dreams, though I couldn't hold onto them. They were like a dance of thoughts, showing me many options. I could choose more than one because they can coexist. I was safe, warm, relaxed, relieved. I went swimming this morning, feeling better.

FEBRUARY 13

Dealing with my marriage is wearing, painful work. Last night I felt horrible when I went to bed: a lump, a failure, overwhelmed. I thought I'd have to call up Ann for an emergency "count your blessings" session. But this morning I woke up feeling wonderful, as if a cloud had been lifted from me.

I called Ted. I asked what prompted him to phone Gail as it's been such a long time since we've had any contact. He said nothing prompted him. He hadn't been able to make an appointment at the time of his conference, but he had hoped there would be another occasion for him to be in the city. It became obvious that there wouldn't be, so he was willing to make a special trip. (And if you believe that, you believe in the tooth fairy. It took him a year to realize he wouldn't be here for some other reason? Give me a break.)

I asked him what he hoped to get out of the meeting. He said, "nothing." He was going because Gail asked him to, because she thought it would be beneficial for us to interact and she might want some information from him.

When we've spoken before, he's sounded businesslike, as if we were discussing mortgages. (I bet he gets more emotional over his mortgage.) This evening he sounded antagonistic, but who knows what he felt. I'm not sure if I care. Well the truth is that I do. When he last called Gail, I was pleasantly surprised that he expressed interest in bettering our relationship. Now he isn't. I don't want to have a relationship with Ted either, but I'm hurt because he cares nothing for me.

I wonder if he's relieved that I told Mum and Dad about Mama so that he can be allied with everyone else against me. It lets him off the hook, at least as far as they're concerned. They can all focus on that issue and ignore Ted's abuse.

FEBRUARY 15

I'm comfortably tired. I went swimming tonight and had the pool to myself most of the time. It was wonderful. Oh, it's so good to be alive. I just changed the sheets and my bed is clean and welcoming.

FEBRUARY 23

My life is starting to take a shape that engages me in a world of brightness and joy. Why, then, am I bursting into tears every couple of minutes? My head hurts. I am depressed and sad. What is happening to me? I am sabotaging myself by procrastinating and being less physically active. Maybe it's just a case of two steps forward and one backward.

In *Becoming Your Own Parent*,[1] I read that the abused child's true self hides for protection while a false self surfaces to take care of business. When I imagine myself emerging with wings of colour, I am really picturing the emergence of my true self, the self that radiates energy, singing in the great song of life.

FEBRUARY 24

I dreamt there was a man and his father and a young woman who'd been shattered trying to protect a child, the daughter, many years before. The young woman's mind was blank in a lot of areas, but suddenly present in others — almost like an idiot-savante. The man wanted to go out with me but I was afraid the same thing would happen again. I thought the only reason he wanted to ask me out is that I was the only one who would accept. Then I was reenacting the whole thing. I was walking with a little girl. I waved and called to her

---

1 Dennis Wholey, *Becoming Your Own Parent* (New York: Doubleday, 1988).

father "Dad! Dad!" I wanted him to help me protect her. I was scared. I realized it was too late. Something bad was going to happen. I ran with her and then told her to run by herself, hoping to take on the attackers while she got away, but it was too late. We were surrounded. I woke up, terrified.

When I talked to Gail about the dream (and it was so hard, I burst into tears at one point), it was entirely clear to me. The man and his father were Ted/Eugene and Dad. The little girl who'd been lost long ago was me and the woman who was shattered was me. Because in some ways I was like an idiot-savante: well-developed in certain areas and completely blank in others. The reenactment I feared was exactly what happened in my marriage. The child I was protecting at the end of the dream was me and the man I was calling to was my father. I was asking for his help and protection, which I didn't get. The ways I tried to protect the child in the dream were how I tried to protect myself: by running away, by hiding the child. But none of it worked. I was abused.

FEBRUARY 25

I had the nicest dream: I met a man named Bob through Janet's sister. He was from the country, thirty-five, dark hair, comfortable face, sturdy build. He was steady and considerate. We went dancing. After we'd known each other for a while, Bob said we should get married. We were hugging and joking around. It felt warm and good. I said yes.

FEBRUARY 28

I've thought that I didn't deserve to be abused. I'm now starting to realize that I deserve to feel good and enjoy my body. I deserve to be treated well. Gail says this is what she means by forgiving myself for my marriage.

MARCH 4

I'm afraid of my physicalness, sexuality and intimacy. Mama experienced her sexuality strongly. She believed herself beautiful.

Would I be ugly inside, like her, if I felt the same? Or would I become crazy the way she was?

MARCH 5

Another woman's work in group reminded me of being abused by Ted. When I started to cry, one of the therapists held me while I trembled, encouraging me to cry freely. After I was done, she sat beside me with her arms around me. It was a wonderful experience, the first time in my life that I have cried so long and freely, comforted and cared for.

MARCH 9

Working at home around Eugene, there was no space that was mine. Every surface was covered by Eugene's newspapers, moldy books, accounting paper filled with his monotony games or baseball stats, scraps of paper from cutouts of amphibians. I had to squeeze by the couch to the photocopier, squeeze by the table to the bureau to get a file, squeeze back to the photocopier, oops forgot to reprint a schedule, squeeze by the table to the computer and yank the chair past the wires and Eugene's crumpled papers on the floor; frazzled and smiling so I wouldn't spark an explosion from Eugene, who was sitting on my papers.

This week I went out and bought an office chair and tables. Both the chair and the tables are adjustable for height. For the first time in my life, I can sit with my feet flat on the floor and my chin isn't on the table. I have a work area. Even the cats walk around the edges of my work area instead of flopping into the middle of my papers. I feel so pampered when I'm working. I look out the window at spruce trees and birds nesting. Isn't that terrific?

MARCH 13

Anna says I don't have to be on my own in my journey. Though it's mine alone to walk and feel, other people can walk with and comfort me.

MARCH 14

Gail says she isn't convinced that I am committed to going on. That shakes me up. I haven't written any poetry for six weeks.

Whatever stops me from writing is dangerous.

I am determined to write whatever comes. I will see it through.

MARCH 15

I had the most wonderful dream last night: there were a bunch of people in an actors' workshop. They were pretending to work instead of really working. I thought they were boring. One person was taking up a lot of time. Someone with several crutches came along wanting her turn, and then another person. I was watching them and I started to fly. I said, "Come on. Look at me. I'm flying and you can fly too." They were so mired in their boredom, they didn't see. I sang, "Look at me, here I am, way above the clouds, watch me everyone, I'm flying." I said again, "You can fly, too. Think wonderful thoughts. Flowers. Music. God. You don't have to go through it alone. Comfort." And they started to fly too.

It's 4:00 a.m. I'm a wrung out dishrag, numb if you want to know, in the "I can't feel any more" zone. Though I felt really good after teaching tonight, I couldn't sleep. Finally I gave in and went to work on my poem.

I was horrified by what I wrote. It was so self-hating. I went to bed, feeling torn up. What could I do if that was in me? It was like a poison. I kept thinking over and over that this hatred is misplaced. It belongs to the people who abused me, not to my body. I began to get that "memory in my body" sensation I've had every since I was a kid. I really wanted to remember so I could let go of the self-hatred.

I prayed for strength. I told myself I was safe. When I began to hyperventilate, I made myself breathe slowly. I was holding my teddy bear because at some point I cried and lay down holding it.

I remembered being asleep, waking up to Ted masturbating me. I came and he said at that moment, "I do something for you and you do something for me. Say yes." I said yes, without understanding. Then I saw his penis, erect, sticking out of his pyjamas. I became terrified, crying, screaming no, shaking my head, and kicking because

I knew a bad thing was going to happen. He stifled my screams with his hand, and then his mouth. I lost all sensation as if I had no body. At that instant the connection between my mind and body snapped.

Hatred for the body that was vulnerable to violation, to pain, to indignity, buried this memory in ice. My body went numb with cold, but the ice saved me from a shock I couldn't bear.

The force of life that drew me from ice into burning reality has brought back the pain of that memory, has brought back disgust, helplessness, rage, strength, pleasure, sexuality — all that is in my body, awake to feeling and knowledge. I am body and mind, left hand and right, blessings and hurt. I forgive myself.

FOUR

Beginning

XXI

The Sea of Change

Recovery is an experience of rebirth. As we proceed, labour intensifies, requiring great effort to confront the past on deep levels and to face the future with newborn wholeness.

Working at this level demanded a lot of me. It was emotionally and physically draining and to get through it, I needed all my strength. I couldn't spare the energy that I had previously lost in the split between my body and mind. All my life this split had deprived me of feelings, perceptions and vigour. When the abuse abated, or I got away from it, the split narrowed and I was stronger, more adventuresome. I took better care of my body. I enjoyed parts of my life I avoided at other times. For instance, after my brother left home, I made male friends, joined the drama club and took part in folk dancing. Yet, narrow or wide, the split was necessary for my survival as long as I was being abused or unable to handle my memories.

Three years of therapy taught me to remove myself from abusers. I learned to feel and remember, slowly letting go of the past as I dealt with it, filling my life with good things instead. Unlike the temporary narrowing I'd experienced before, the split healed in places where I reclaimed the feelings and memories that divided me. Just like integrating other parts of my being, healing the split between my body and mind gave me strength to proceed until I found myself in advanced labour.

The winter of 1989 was a season of slogging work. I did not rush forward. At times I simply stopped for a breather, needing a push to get me going again. Yet, slow as it was, I forgave myself for being crushed by Eugene, for being female like my grandmother and, at last, for suffering my brother's violence. Forgiveness brought the realization that my body was not an "it," not something separate. By spring

211

I knew myself as one person with united energies. I was ready to work in the depths of my past, getting set to explore what the future could hold for my true adult self, born out of that labour.

Memories of what happened to my body as "it," though an important "it," were now memories of what happened to me. I saw them in a different light, sharper, more immediate, especially the times I'd been most disconnected. These were the times of shock and disaster: moving into my grandmother's room, my brother's violence, the worst of Eugene's abuse. My innermost feelings about these times began to emerge, demanding a voice for the years I was so silent. I was scared. At this deep level I again had to relearn to speak, to overcome my fears of speaking. The silence was years long and had been lifesaving. Speaking out was recent. I had only three years of practice, but I trusted the supportive people in my life and I trusted myself. I knew that the more deeply I exorcised the past, the more my life improved. I saw rightness in how far I'd come over the course of therapy and I felt how much more I enjoyed my life. With this sense of rightness, I felt like I was proceeding at breakneck speed. I realized that the outcome of this work was growing up, about which I was still uncertain, but that seemed far away. Occasionally old fears resurged to temper my pace, comforting me with assurances of childishness. Nevertheless, concentrating on where I was rather than where I was headed, I galloped on toward adulthood.

1989

MARCH 22

Last night I dreamt that Gail was pouring silver chain links into a basket to represent all the things I was going on to. Looking at the basket, I suddenly got scared, overwhelmed by the quantity of silver. Then I was climbing the alpine path between the sea of change and the sea of strange.

MARCH 25

I bought some lovely "spring rain" bath beads to pamper myself.

MARCH 26

It's a beautiful day. I slept in and am now writing in bed, looking out at the trees, listening to the birds singing, revelling in the peace, cleanliness and prettiness of my bedroom.

MARCH 27

I thought of something important while I was sleeping. I am now going back and saying no to the abuse, which I couldn't as a child. I must do that for the child I was because she was helpless and I am not.

MARCH 28

I am so glad Gail's my therapist. I feel full of love, affection, trust and faith in her, a relaxed feeling that I can depend on her and it'll be okay. Isn't that wonderful?!

MARCH 31

CAT AGAINST SKIN

Afternoon nap naked
cat stretched
against my chest and belly,
paws on my arms
and in the crook of my legs.
His fur makes my skin feel like silk,
my breasts and belly beautiful
with cat against my skin.

APRIL 1

While I was swimming, I realized what my definition of success is: to grow into a woman of vitality, love, wisdom and humour, to be all of myself, fulfilling my potential, becoming the old woman of my dreams.

APRIL 2

I swam thirty laps today!

APRIL 4

Gail reassures me that she will not kick me out of therapy. (Yay!!)

APRIL 14

I'm not feeling terribly wonderful today. As a matter of fact, I'm sitting with my teddy bear on my lap, resting my chin on its head. The odd thing these days is that when I'm not feeling dreadful, I'm very energetic and getting all my work done. No procrastinating, which is amazing.

Well, there's this six year old kid in me who's been in the new house a few months, still reeling from the shock of being thrown to Mama. She is dying to speak and is terrified because she learned to save herself by being quiet around adults. Whenever I see Gail lately, this kid part comes out. There are a lot of silences because she is so scared to talk, though she needs to, and feels safe enough with Gail and with me as the adult self to emerge. For a while afterward, I feel like that six-year-old: cold, nauseous and flushed, hurt and scared. The feelings dissipate, but they return periodically. Yesterday I bought toys for the little me: crayons, colouring books, bubbles, plasticine, paints. I didn't get to play at home without a sense of danger when I was a child, but I can give myself that pleasure now.

APRIL 18

I got the Canada Council grant! I just couldn't believe it. I didn't expect to hear from them for another month. I was terrified when I opened the letter. I read it and screamed! I called everyone under the sun. I feel wonderful!

APRIL 19

I'm sad. It's Pesakh tonight and I hurt. I'm glad I'm going to sleep over at Janet's.

I tend to think of normalcy as being even keeled and happy, but it isn't. It's happy and sad. Health is simply not being weighed down, tied up, frustrated, limited a thousandfold by the past. It's being free to be ourselves now, with ups and downs and some bumps from the past.

APRIL 25

My reactions in therapy lately remind me of when I first began: the difficulty I have talking, the internal struggles, the bigger place therapy has in my life right now. When I began therapy, the largest part of me was taken up by the kid in me, but it was covered up by a pseudo-adult that concealed and coped with the kid. So I reacted as the child, but dealt with it as the pseudo-adult. Now a large part of me really is grown-up but when I walk into my sessions, the kid part comes out quickly, while the adult takes a back seat. I've lost the pseudo-adult responses, though I've tried to recapture them. I can't withdraw the way I used to, slamming a door in Gail's face. I feel lost and scared, not knowing how to deal with these kid reactions, nor how Gail will respond. She is gentle with the kid in me, encouraging her to come out. For my part, I trust Gail enough to talk to her with the child's voice, to be the child openly, despite some struggles and fear. I feel lighter in heart. A bit scared too, still a little sick and of all things — delighted. I feel as though I've come full circle to a better place: the spiral.

In group tonight we began the spring session by spending some time writing about a memory. Here is what I wrote: "This is a safe place where no one can hurt me. It's okay to be little here. It's okay to be me.

Now that I am six, I share a room with Mama. She is big and I am small. She comes to my bed even though her bed is a very big bed and mine is small. I wake up and she is there. I feel sick. I am scared."

Anna held me while I cried. She warmed and comforted me.

APRIL 29

LOOK AND LISTEN

You look and listen to me. Why do you act so stupid, as if you can't see, as if you can't hear? I scream and scream in my sleep. Do you come? Do you say "Is something wrong?" No. You let me scream and be scared. You let me alone. You leave me with Mama.

Her bed creaks when she gets up. My bed creaks when she lies down. It wakes me up, scared. Where are you? I cry, "I want my mother," and Mama chokes me quiet. Where is my mother? She's asleep with the baby. She doesn't care if Mama hurts me. You don't care about me at all. I wish I was dead. I go Gone.

The Gone place sparkles with all colours. The Gone place hums. It smells warm, like my mother on Sunday mornings in her bed. I want my mother.

I am Here. Mama is heavy, squishing me, smelling hot, hot, and bad. Her face is crazy, all twisted. Her mouth is wet and she kisses me here and there, tickly and squirmy. I can't breathe. Her breasts are on my face. I am dizzy. I go Gone.

I am Here. Mama is in her bed. I sleep and I scream and nobody listens.

I want you to look and listen to me. See where Mama hurt me. She hurts me outside and inside. She kisses me and it isn't nice. She puts her tongue inside my mouth and other places. She touches my vagina. You showed me my vagina. You have one and I have one and so does the baby, that's what you said. It is sensitive and you have to be gentle when you wash it. People aren't supposed to touch it. How come you let Mama touch it and hurt me there? Why don't you stop her? I want you to stop her.

You don't love me or you would stop her. I hate you. You're a bad mother. If you were a good mother you would care about me. You would hold me when I hurt instead of leaving me to hurt by myself with my doll. All you care about is the new baby. You want me to leave you alone and be quiet. I am too much for you. You don't have *Koikh* (strength) for me. I act quiet but I am mad. I want to scream: "Put down that baby. You're my mother. You're supposed to take care

216 • FOUR: BEGINNING

of *me*. Stop Mama from hurting me! Make her go away! She is bad. Kick her out!"

I don't yell because you want me to be quiet. I love you and I want to be good so you'll love me too. I look and look at you, hoping that you'll look at me and see what I need you to do, what I need from you. But you don't see me. If you looked in my eyes, you'd see all the hurting and the want that is there. How much I want you to love me and hold me, and make the hurting go away. But you don't want me around you. You make me sleep with Mama. You push me away. That hurts me so I want to die. Why don't you love me? Why don't you want me? I need to be wanted just like I am, not like a quiet doll. I'm not quiet. I make noise. I jump up and down. But you don't like that. You don't like me. Well I don't need you either. I don't need anybody, so there.

I sit on my bed, quiet. I look out the window and I talk to the trees and my doll. I am sad. It isn't true that I don't need anybody. It isn't true at all. I pretend that the trees and my doll are all I need, but they can't talk to me. They don't have ears. They can't make nice when I hurt. They can't hold me when I cry. I need a real person to listen. I need somebody who looks at the hurt, and cares and holds me.

MAY 2

It is hard for me to accept Anna's comfort. In part I want to run from her because crying and allowing her to hold me seems too *khutzpedik* (nervy). It is so unfamiliar to be a mother's child, like the other women in group, entitled to attention. It is so unlike my family.

Dear God, please help me bear my feelings and put them into something that is a growing thing. The naked truth in child pain is so stark and bleak, the child so innocent and vulnerable. Help me be the child. Help me protect her so she can speak, knowing that the grown-up me can bear her feelings, wants her to speak, honours her voice. She is me and I am her. We are the same.

MAY 4

I had a good dream about being six years old, comforted by Gail. Then I had a sad dream about a convict who was forced to make pornographic films. It made me realize that I have to deal with the sexual sensations I experienced during the abuse. I have to face my reactions to that.

MAY 5

A dream last night: Mama admitted that sometimes she'd hit me too hard. Dad was in his car beside us. He heard Mama with tears in his eyes, but it made no difference. He still couldn't believe me. Then I woke up feeling sad.

MAY 12

I picked up my new car today: burgundy and beautiful. I love it! The radio is jazzy. Getting this car repairs so much. Besides Eugene's sliming, the old car held the memories of my being refused a loan, twice, even with my employers' good word, Eugene unable to cosign, and that being a secret. The humiliation, frustration and fear connected with leasing my first car was typical of my marriage. Now I've left a chunk of that behind. I feel respectable, a solid citizen. I own a car and a bank loan! Hurray!!

MAY 21

It's such a beautiful day: the world looks freshly painted, the air smells green. I woke up early and washed the kitchen. The living room is freshly vacuumed, so I'm in a palace with my chariot waiting outside. I'm thinking again about my dream of the two evils. If I can get through them, I will recover the lost poetry. This lovely morning with Snowball against my knee, I feel hopeful. The evils seem shadowy. The good — poetry and laughter and fun — is in my hands and around my neck, like tickling flickering colours.

I'm actually getting paid to write. Imagine that! It's so amazing I can't quite take it in. I feel like a dream I thought was beyond my reach has suddenly become reality. Hurray for me and the long road!

MAY 27

I'm amazed at how good I feel, especially because yesterday I was in so much pain I could hardly bear it. I was frustrated, in one of my "this has been going on forever and will never end" moods.

I've been "cleaning house" all week. I decided that half my problems come about because I allow myself to be put in situations I really don't want and then I hide my head in the sand, worrying, refusing to deal with it until it blows up in my face, which I've been anticipating and fretting over all along. My life will be simpler and a lot more pleasant if I just face up to those things and get rid of them, instead of hiding. So that's what I did. I got out of some work and personal plans with which I didn't want to be involved, and discussed my upcoming peer review with the Institute. I understand the procedure now and have made convenient arrangements with them, so that's a load off my mind. I also told Mum and Dad I've received a grant to write. I felt awful hiding it as if it were a terrible secret, like the incest was. I'm glad I told them, another weight off my chest, and I'm glad I found a way to talk about it without discussing the subject matter of my book. That would just cause heartache for all of us.

Last night I did a rough outline of my book, and on Monday I'll work out a schedule. This is it. I'm living out my dream, given the opportunity to prove myself. Will I? There's the risk. Tomorrow Janet and I are going to the country for the day. I'm really looking forward to it. It's nice to have a future to look forward to. Who knows what's going to happen? It's so exciting. All kinds of new and wonderful things seem to be waiting for me. It's in my power to get there. I think.

MAY 28

What an absolutely wonderful day. I took the scenic route to Kleinberg. I saw a turtle sunbathing in a creek, fed grass to a goat — such gentle, soft lips. I toured the art gallery, had a picnic lunch, visited the town and walked in the woods on the gallery grounds. It was a sunny, cloudless day, perfect. I got a bit of a burn and that just makes it feel like summer. I saw one painting, called "Dependency," of a woman with a baby on her back, surrounded by a circle of vines, leaves, berries and birds. Janet called it "Survival." Right.

JUNE 1

Tuesday in group was amazing. I was dying to work, though I had no clear idea what about. I just knew I needed to deal with "a darkness so deep and thick," which was as far as I could get in the poem I'm writing.

I asked Anna to sit beside me. I was shaking. I had no words. Anna told me to let myself shake, "Your body remembers." She said I could not be comforted when I was abused and asked me if I wanted comfort now. Yes. From her? Yes.

Anna put her arms around me and I clung to her for dear life, crying. I knew where I was. I could feel Anna, her cheek, her neck, her arms around me. I could hear her tell me over and over that she had me and she was here. At the same time I was in the past. It was as if I was living the scream inside my head. I was crying, making little noises, scared breathing, moving, rocking, stamping my bare foot with volcanic emotion. I had no thoughts except that I was helpless to stop it. I had no words, no images, no tears. At last I felt a change in my crying, and I had a clear picture of Mama walking from my bed to hers. It was only then that I realized I had been reliving the abuse, expressing the terror and pain I couldn't when I was little. The difference now is that I was held safe and lovingly, comforted. After I stopped crying, I sat with my head on Anna's shoulder for a while, clutching her hand, trembling a little, still, with her arm around me.

I've always been scared to death of getting lost in a memory. It's a wonderful thing to remember how I was there, in the past, and yet I was also here. The safety, comfort, and love, here, enabled me to live through it differently so that some part of the pain is laid to rest, and some part of my little kid feels loved and happy.

JUNE 10

In group I slid right into the same place I was last week, but I fought it all the way. Being so deeply emotional and fighting it so hard gave me a stomach ache. I felt miserable with the pain and terror and unexpressed desolation. I called Alma after group and she reassured me that if I let go, I wouldn't feel anything more than I could handle.

I felt better after that, lying quietly on the couch, thinking. Over the last three years I've been climbing down the strands of a web. The centre of the web is the dark place, where I did the deep work in group last week. Anna says I am experiencing rebirth; then I wonder if the dark place is the womb or the birth canal.[1]

JUNE 21

I'm whacked out with a cold, but get this — *Fireweed*[2] is going to publish one of my poems!

JUNE 25

I hurt so bad, I can't stand it. I feel such a need to be held and comforted. I feel lost and alone.

JUNE 26

I've been getting a lot of work done and having many nice times, but also times of terrible nausea and headaches, especially before sleeping and on waking up. I get relief by becoming aware of my intense anger and terrible hurt and letting it out. This morning I punched pillows, hit the couch with my tennis racket and cried. Talking to friends helps too, and swimming. I got some reassurance from Ann about it being all right to be so mad. She said if I weren't angry, I'd be living my parents' idea of "cured — it never happened." At any rate I feel good now and did have such a fun time swimming this morning. I'm teaching myself the crawl.

JUNE 27

Oh this is torture. Each time I go to the dark place with Anna or Gail, it's for a longer time, deeper, more conscious and vocal. God

---

1 The dark place is the deep recess of being, the core. At first it was frightening as I felt the abuse with an intensity I'd never imagined. But it was the dark place that gave me the strength to encounter profound feelings and knowledge. It is the place of mystery and creativity, awesome in its transforming, impelling power.

2 *Fireweed, A Feminist Quarterly* 29 (Toronto, 1989) 86.

this is hard. But each time I feel and express the pain, there is less of it. One day it will be finished.

JUNE 28
I didn't expect group ending to hit me so hard. I have that kicked in the stomach sensation I used to get when Gail went on holiday, feeling abandoned and in despair, knowing that horror is coming. I feel so close to the past, I'm horribly anxious and sick trying to keep myself present because it's frightening to be there alone. I'll try to do as many pleasant things as I can today.

JUNE 29
I'm so glad I feel better. When I saw Gail today, I felt like I was in the dark place almost right away. It was different. Instead of terror or pain, I cried with sorrow.

JULY 2
What a gorgeous day — warm, sunny, dry. The pool was wonderful. I swam thirty-two laps. I've had such a craving for activity the last couple of days. I feel like my body is bursting with energy, just dancing. Though at first I was hard hit by group ending for the summer, I'm glad to have the break. Group is so intense. Sometimes I feel like I'm in an incest ghetto. I look forward to expanding my horizons.

Last night I dreamt I was talking to Eugene on the phone. He called to tell me that he loved me. I yelled back, "Well I don't love you and I never loved you. I didn't know what love is." Then I woke up.

JULY 3
If I reacted so strongly to group ending, I wonder how I'll handle Gail's holiday. I am *petrified*. I feel like the little kid part of me is in hysterics.

JULY 7
I'm mad at Gail because I'm growing up — rapidly. I've been angry with Gail before, but I've never allowed her in so deep, never

trusted so much in her caring for me as I have in going to the dark place. It seems that at each level I have to reacquaint myself with the same truths, making them mine again. If the dark place is the centre of being, then my difficulty has been to take in this truth about love and anger at my core: my anger won't annihilate anyone I care for, nor will those I feel cared by annihilate me because I am angry.

JULY 8

I dreamt that a voice said I was at the crossroads, but I could stay there as long as I wanted.

XXII

At the Crossroads

JULY 9

TOUCH ME AND DANCE
In my house, love was thin ice
shattered by my voice,
never knowing where I'd fall through
to thrash about
gulping shards
searching for a hold, right word, right tone.

I still breathe scared past broken glass
waiting to fall
though here the ice has melted.

I am naked with myself in water
where a stone's throw ripples, nothing more.
Breathe deep and shout welcome.
Drink and be free.
Love is water.
Touch me and dance
like waves of the sea.

"Touch Me and Dance" was a gift from my core to my conscious mind, providing a glimpse of joyful freedom not yet mine, but within my reach. This glimpse gave me the will to examine the constraints that still bound me. I didn't have to think very hard: my brother's name lit up in glaring neon. Though I'd remembered Ted's violence and was aware that he'd raped me, I hadn't dealt with it. The odd time I referred to it in therapy, I called it "that thing that happened, you know, when my brother woke me up." I thought that having remembered it, my task was finished, and swept the memory back under the carpet. I didn't even tell Ann, the sharer of my deepest thoughts, about it.

Though I wasn't finished with the memory, it did mark a new stage in my recovery. Here I found a different view of therapy. I saw that it was not a straight march through my life, picking up pieces of me from A to Z the way I'd assumed. That assumption was based on a lifetime that had been heavy on logic and short on feelings. Logic gave me a sense of safety and control, which I applied to everything, including therapy. I first approached therapy like school: read the right books, do my homework conscientiously, get an A and be cured. Experience quickly showed me this wasn't realistic, but I continued to look for the formula that would make therapy controllable, predictable and simple. The notion that I could trust myself to grow in my own time and way was, at first, unimaginable.

Over three years the balance between logic and feelings had gradually shifted. I discovered that emotions weren't governable by logic and that life couldn't be overcome with a battle strategy or tied down by a timetable. Learning I could control my actions and protect myself, I had less need to control my feelings and surroundings. I found that I could meet what came my way and grow from it. Believing in myself led me to look inward for an understanding of recovery. I realized that it was a process of healing on ever deeper levels, a web, not a march. I suspected that somewhere in the process I'd have to lift the carpet and sweep it clean. "Touch Me and Dance" gave me the impetus I needed. After reading the poem to Gail, I told her I wanted to deal with Ted's abuse again. Instead of referring to "that thing, you know," I began to talk about rape.

Even with my vision of the web, my simple A to Z attitude didn't disappear overnight. Instead the recovery formula became to work through successive layers to the centre. Having reached the six year old kid at my centre, I concluded that I would just do the same kind of work until I retrieved all the abused parts of me still there. I'd vanquish my grandmother, my brother, and Eugene, and head off into the wild blue yonder. My experience of working in the dark place was a positive one, each time feeling bits of the past laid finally to rest. Intense as the work was, it was eased by my ability to take in support at that level just as intensely, drinking it in like I'd been dying of thirst. Crying in Anna's arms, her cheek soft against mine, or curled beside Gail, her hand on my back, cheering me on, I felt comforted and loved. That comfort and love, received in the core of my being where I'd been abused and denied, was a miracle. I didn't realize that I had recovered from different aspects of my life to varying degrees. When I turned toward the memory of my brother's violence, I assumed I'd deal with it in the same way, rewarded by the same miracle. I couldn't. Just beginning to probe my feelings about it, I wasn't ready to open myself to the core, whether to look at my past or take in support.

I missed the deep comfort I'd so recently found. Feeling disappointed and uncertain, I was unaware that it was time to go more slowly. I looked for stumbling blocks where there were none, only the natural process of dealing with a part of my life newly recovered. Rather than respect my change of pace, I tried to topple these nonexistent blocks, effectively slowing myself down anyway. I felt frustrated and bad about myself. It was a familiar trap, trying to force my will on the uncontrollable, feeling like a failure when I couldn't. The difference was that I didn't fall into it as deeply as I once would have. Despite my worrying and frustration, I was doing the work I needed to.

The crossroads was a place of remembering and accepting my memories. Where I took them — back under the carpet, stopping my life, or upfront, dealing with them so I could go on — was a decision I had yet to make.

I wasn't sure about what lay ahead. I would have to decide if I really wanted to get there, which meant facing what "there" was all about, and defining it for myself. In my spring gallop I just ignored the wild blue yonder I was moving toward. Now, suddenly, it seemed so much closer. The crossroads allowed me to pause and get my bearings. As my unconscious assured me, always so much gentler and wiser than my conscious mind, I could stay there until I was ready to go on.

*   *   *   *   *

JULY 13

I told Ann yesterday that Ted had raped me. When I told her, I really accepted it.

I lay down this afternoon for a nap and started shaking. I remembered then the details of the rape, the peculiar look of Ted's pyjama string hanging down below his penis, jutting out dark over the white pyjama band, hand over my mouth. I kick my legs furiously until he pins me with his knees, saying "remember you said yes," and I pause in shock, mouth on mine, arching my back and screaming as he goes in, feeling broken, falling limp, lying half-curled on my side like a broken thing as he leaves, saying, "remember you said, yes," throwing up.

JULY 14

My anxiety is at fever pitch. Breathe. I called Gail. I don't know how she can help me but I just want to know she's there.

I went over to Janet's and swam sixty-one laps. If this continues, I'm going to be in great shape. Her company and the swimming made me feel a lot better. I was able to feel sad and mad, releasing some of that instead of being gripped by anxiety.

JULY 18

I'm so angry and I don't understand why. I feel bad-tempered and negative. I just want to gnash my teeth.

JULY 20

DELIVERY
My voice died when my brother raped me,
a broken music box spinning circles of grief
in three notes:
the gasp of blame,
of legs forced apart,
the scream of breaking silenced
like a birth stopped at the entrance to life.
This circle circumscribes me
my screams unleashed will push me
deliver me with tenderness and trust,
touching and touched,
my voice reborn
in communion.

JULY 22
I feel alive and unencumbered. I want to shout! Oh frabjous[1] joy!

JULY 23
Everyone else seems to think that my present difficulty with Gail's holiday has to do with accepting how far I've come. I seem to be having more trouble working and communicating in therapy at times. I'm sick to death of therapy running my life. I want to run it.

JULY 28
So I don't see Gail now for two weeks. I don't feel terrible about that.

I've been working in therapy at high fever pitch for a couple of months. Exhausting. Yet when I don't get to that deep a level, I feel let down and unsatisfied. The deep work is necessary, relieving, exciting in its intensity and leads where I need to go, but it's also tiresome. I need to remind myself what life is all about: living, not

---

1 From the poem, "Jabberwockey" by Lewis Carroll.

therapy. Warmth and love isn't a reward for pain. It helps me heal but it exists outside of pain. Excitement does not equal intensity, danger and chaos. Excitement is fun, challenge, new experiences and feeling good. Healing, I can enjoy loving intimacy without the pain of abuse as a backdrop that casts a pall over everything.

JULY 30

When I finish therapy, what will fill the gap in time, concentration, thought, emotion, focus? It's exciting and scary. What will become of me? The answer isn't the blank it once was, though I'm not ready to articulate the flickering images. For now it's time to take a break, relax and enjoy myself.

AUGUST 9

Sometimes I wonder if therapy wasn't sent into my life to teach me patience.

AUGUST 14

I don't know what's going on with me this evening. I walked into the bedroom with my journal, bursting into tears of "I don't want to do anything any more. This is stupid." I saw Gail today and it was fine. So no problem, right? Wrong. I feel frustrated and I don't know why. I wondered at first if it was because I expected too much, but I don't think so, or not much, anyhow. Could it be that somehow I'm saying what I think I should instead of what I need to in my sessions?

AUGUST 15

Happy Birthday! Sparklers on cheesecake, presents, hugs, wine, swimming — a lovely day.

AUGUST 19

I feel sad, reminded in sexual enjoyment of the preponderance of sexual abuse. Pleasant sex, consideration, holding, that isn't much to expect. But it seems so difficult and that makes me sad.

I had a dream last night about a deaf woman singing in a play. I curled up and cried, banging my fists and feet noiselessly because I didn't want to disturb the play. It seemed to go on forever and I couldn't stand it. I wanted Anna. Then she was there, putting her hand on my back. The touch seemed to burn into my soul.

AUGUST 22
Because I've allowed some people in quite deeply, there's a last gasp of the old me. I feel tremendous fear and panic as I get down to the centre and I am revealed naked.

AUGUST 25
Another yucky discussion about seeing Gail once, instead of twice, a week.

AUGUST 29
As time has gone on since my initial memory of being raped, more and more details have come back to me vividly; and of course with them surge the feelings. I was miserable today, swamped with hurting, anger, memory, burning in my stomach. Not even swimming helped. I told Janet I wished I could stand on the balcony and scream. She suggested I scream under water. I did. I stood on the bottom of the pool and screamed with all my might. It made me giggle because it felt so good, the release and the bubbly sensation. Screaming under water sounds like whales singing. I want more!

I love water. In water I feel so safe and alive, surrounded by love. I still feel some tension, the pressure of feelings that have yet to come out, but I also feel good. I am satisfied with myself and glad.

SEPTEMBER 1
It makes no sense, but somehow I believe my feeling sexual was punished by Ted's and Eugene's abuse. I don't like that. It makes me angry with them. But I also feel ashamed, even though they were the ones who put the idea into my head by telling me that I asked for it. This shame underlies the negative messages that have been constantly running through my mind lately, like a background noise. It makes me want to run away. Then I'm afraid that Gail will kick me out. It is hard to accept guilt I don't want to feel. I wish I were beyond it.

But I'm better off facing my guilt so I can go past it, than denying my guilt and getting stuck in it.

SEPTEMBER 6

I'm sad. I decided yesterday to suggest to Gail that I start seeing her once a week on October 9. Gail thinks that seeing her twice a week has become an issue of dependence. The kid part of me went wingy when she brought it up.

While I was washing the dishes, I realized something. Gail can't force me to grow up. That's my choice. No matter how much I care about Gail, or anyone else, it's not enough to make me do what I don't want.

Remembering the rape brought me to another crossroads. It connects with difficult aspects of my marriage. Why should I deal with this? Why should I feel this pain? What's in it for me?

If I continue, the limitations that are not part of my human limitations, but are self-imposed as a result of the abuse in my life, will simply not exist. These limitations relate to work, intimacy, trust, sexuality, and more I'm sure. My writing too, always my writing. For the sake of my writing, if nothing else, I'll go on. That makes me cry. I'll go on though I'm scared. Going on means growing up.

Growing up means giving up those self-imposed limitations and accepting the limitations of being human in this world of ours. A world of wonder. A world of horror. A world of everyday tasks and pleasures. A finite world where people die, all of us. A world of other limited people.

What do I get for all this giving up and acceptance?

I get to make my corner of the world my own in my time. I get to sing, no holds barred, in the great song of life. I get to love and be loved. I get to be me, occupied by me, instead of by tendrils of abuse that invade my life with nausea, fears and depression. I get to reclaim all of me with all the power a unified me has.

I will never be everything I wish I could. But I can be my vision of the old woman: happy, loving, beloved, a source of life. I can use and develop my gifts. I can relish my femaleness, my sexuality and physicalness.

XXIII

Beyond Survival

By defining adulthood and what it had to offer me, I took charge of my direction and left the crossroads. My decision to go on was a two-pronged commitment: to freedom from self-imposed constraints and to my growth. Freedom lay in facing the pain of my brother's violence and my marriage. Growth required me to work toward the vision of the adult life I wanted to develop. I was living the germ of this vision with work, relationships and activities that fit my likes and dislikes, my strengths and weaknesses. It was a solid start, but just a seed as yet, because I had devoted so much effort to recovering from the past. It was time to channel some of that energy into expanding my life here and now.

To widen my horizons, I had to overcome the fears that made me cling to my familiar routine. I was afraid of being abused again. I was afraid of reaching for what I wanted and failing. I was afraid of the feelings aroused in me as I realized how good life could be, and by contrast, how bad it had been. A routine built around therapy had brought me to the point where I could handle these fears. But what had once been beneficial was becoming a rut, consuming energy and commitment I needed to spread my wings. When Gail brought this to my attention, suggesting that I see her once instead of twice a week, I felt threatened. I did not hear it as a caring push toward independence, I heard alarm bells warning that I was being tossed into the cold sea and had better kick and fight to hold on.

Gail's move to reduce the amount of time I saw her threw me into a panic. The only pushing I had known did not propel me toward independence, but pushed me away. From my viewpoint, the issue was not whether seeing Gail once a week was better for me, but how to prevent the desertion I anticipated. I tried to convince her that I

232

should continue to see her twice a week. She didn't buy it. Then I had a tantrum, which embarrassed me. Finally I was compliant, hoping that being good would keep Gail from kicking me out. I at least expected that my compliance would shut her up so that I could shove the whole ugly mess back underground.

Much to my annoyance, Gail didn't shut up. She let me know that my reaction was not wiped out by compliance. My agitation indicated that there was something very important to me here, which we needed to discuss. It was a wrenching effort to hear her say that she was thinking about my best interests when I felt like she was taking the first step to deserting me. But with her prodding, backed by my trust, I wrestled with panic to talk about it. Looking at my fear of abandonment allowed me to compare it to reality. I saw that it did not come true. Gail was as concerned and caring as ever. The nest didn't disappear when I tested my wings, a security I'd never known before. This security gave me the confidence to expand my horizons and taught me self-reliance as I looked after myself in new situations.

For years the child in me had been asking, "Who will take care of me?" and the only answer was a lonely echo. Self-reliance would bring a different answer: "I will." This answer contained the knowledge that I was enough.

*   *   *   *   *

SEPTEMBER 8

Gail and I talked again about my seeing her once a week. She says she has no intention of kicking me out of therapy. I came home and burst into tears. I was depressed, then angry. I called Ann and bitched about Gail. She was wonderful, listened and bitched along with me. I pounded a pillow, talked to it, then started crying, hurt again. I feel like I have to see her once a week because I'm not good enough. What else will happen to me if I'm not good enough?

SEPTEMBER 9

A dream: I was reading a note from God. It said that God needs people who do things. I feel good this morning. My sessions with Gail usually wipe me out for the day, so by seeing her once a week, I gain twenty-six days from October to March. Imagine that!

SEPTEMBER 16

It's been such a nice, sleepy day, cold and overcast out, snugly warm in bed. I read, talked on the phone and slept.

SEPTEMBER 17

From *Beyond Survival*[1] by Dow Marmur: "As Jews we understand pain, our own and that of others ... we become conscious of the suffering of all peoples. To alleviate it becomes a religious duty, rooted in personal experience ... The very fact that we have survived points to a purpose. Significantly, the ability to remember our pain and to feel the pain of others leads to an affirmation of life, not a negation of it. ... By contrast, those who seek to escape pain and close their eyes to the pain of others tend to lead miserable lives."

SEPTEMBER 18

I had an internal agenda in dealing with the rape that I simply couldn't meet. Forgetting that it's always taken time to deal with my memories, I came up with all kinds of reasons for being stuck when I really wasn't stuck at all. Yet I felt like I was being bad. I was afraid that Gail would stop seeing me twice a week as a prelude to kicking me out of therapy. I want her assurance that I don't have to be "good" or "bad" for her to care about me, because I don't want to be. I want to be me.

SEPTEMBER 19

Gail says that she cares about me regardless of my behaviour — that's just the way it is and I need to trust and believe that in order to go on with therapy. Hmm.

---

1 Dow Marmur, *Beyond Survival: reflections on the future of Judaism* (London: Darton Longman & Todd, 1982) xv.

SEPTEMBER 27

Gail sitting beside me and putting her arm around me is scary. I like it, but it makes me feel exposed.

This is hard, but I want to write (though suddenly feel very sleepy) because I've continued to have stomach pains on and off this evening. Intimate: "pertaining to inmost thoughts and feelings, very familiar, close, euphemism: of illicit sexual intercourse." Puts my stomach in knots, burning actually, just in the centre of my ribs.

So there is my poem, "Delivery," with enforced terrible intimacy on top, and, on the other side of pain, true caring intimacy. Closeness that feels good. That is respectful. Gentle. Warm. Trustworthy. Constant.

Gail sitting with her arm around me is a good kind of closeness. In the same place it feels nice to be comforted though, I remember being forced into a closeness that was violent, hurting horribly inside my body. First Mama, then Ted, right in the middle of me, breaking me apart inside: very familiar, close, inmost, illicit sexual intercourse. Intimacy. Awful intimacy.

I have a picture of myself as one of the dancers in "Endangered Species,"[2] running, screaming on the post-Holocaust stage, arms flailing in horror.

But it wasn't a stage. It was my life. It wasn't a bomb. It was rape. It was being twelve, barely pubescent, and not any person, but my brother, too big, crushing me in and out. Bastard. Not just the older generation. They all do it. That's all there ever is. Trust? Trust is just waiting for the bad things to happen. Love? That's being disembowelled. You lose everything. Except for silence. You own the words unspoken — that's all that can't be torn limb from limb. "You can tell us anything. We'll always love you." Garbage. "Your brother is so good. You don't know what a brother you have." Only too well. I hate him.

Now there's something different. The experience of difference shows up the hurt beneath my anger. Trust: "to allow a person to be

---

2 "Endangered Species," choreographed by Danny Grossman, The Danny Grossman Dance Company, Toronto.

in a place or to do some action with expectation of safety or without fear of the consequences." Yes. That is why it is so hard to sit with Gail beside me, arm around me, letting down my guard and believing in safety at the very moment I remember being pinned to the bed and raped, trust so betrayed, murdered.

It hurts, and I'm dry-eyed. I only want to sleep. I can't yet cry.

SEPTEMBER 28

I dreamt that I was saying to Mama, "Bad Grandmother," over and over. As I said it, because I said it, she was disappearing slowly from the edges in. Then she went pfft. There was just one drop left, like a tear. It turned to dust and blew away.

OCTOBER 1

It wasn't so long ago that a week was eternity, but now the days seem to fly by.

This weekend was Rosh Hashana. I've been a bit depressed the last few days, just not myself. I think I was more susceptible to the R.H. blues because I went for a physical for the first time in three years, this week. Ann and Janet nagged me into it, but I neglected to tell them that my doctor reminds me of my grandmother and she likes Eugene. Plus the internal brings up memories of being raped. Yuck. It was a horrible experience. My doctor persisted in calling me by my married name and asking about Eugene though she knew I was divorced. Needless to say, I'm not going back to her. I could kick myself for worrying about disappointing Ann and Janet and not cancelling the appointment.

The incident made me realize that it's not only Gail I worry about being "good enough" for, but my friends too. I wonder when I'll trust enough not to worry that I'll suddenly find myself abandoned.

OCTOBER 2

I haven't done this for ages, sit on the window ledge, listening to the wind. I've got candles lit, writing by the soft light, restoring my soul. I love the smell of the fall air. I can feel it where the window's open just a crack.

Evergreens. Cloudy sky. Rooftops. Night colours, dark, interesting, waiting, strong.

OCTOBER 3

I dreamt that I was in a gloomy place, like in the thick of woods, but there were no trees, just rocks and boulders. I had a pickaxe and I was hacking at the rocks to uncover monsters. I woke up scared, but then I thought that at least I was armed.

OCTOBER 5

Before Ted got violent, I felt a kinship with him. I loved and trusted him. He betrayed my trust by abusing me but I didn't realize that. Even though it felt wrong, I believed him when he said he was teaching me or playing a game. His manipulation and deceptiveness now strike me as being heinous because the reality is that I was being abused. But at the time I thought Ted and I were on the same side.

I didn't realize I could say no at first and when I did, I worried about disappointing him and making him mad at me. Still I said no, and he stopped. When he raped me a few months later, I knew he was my enemy. I felt as if he wanted to destroy me. It was completely unexpected. Mama was violent, but not Ted. That wasn't how I knew him. It showed me that you can never believe in anyone.

OCTOBER 9

Ted and Mama were evil. Mum and Dad weren't. I want to be clear about that. But what do you call a collaborator? I don't like the term "silent partner," because it seems to take responsibility away from the abuser and I don't want to do that. The responsibility is all Mama's and Ted's for the evil they did. But Mum and Dad stood by them and they weren't there for me.

OCTOBER 11

I've found that I prefer seeing Gail once a week!

OCTOBER 17

I dreamt that I was in an apartment. The door blew open and I realized it had been ransacked and someone might be inside. I screamed and woke up so terrified I was afraid to open the window, though I was hot.

That was after I went berserk over my computer. It wasn't working properly. I messed around for hours to no avail. I was sure that nothing ever would work for me. Everyone else could have a working computer, but not me. It reminds me of the helplessness and frustration I felt with Eugene. And somehow of Ted. The anger, fear, hurt I was purposefully not thinking about was coming out while I was up until 4:00 in the morning, bawling my eyes out over my computer.

OCTOBER 18

Ted took over where Mama left off. I feel sad and hurt, right in my chest.

OCTOBER 22

I had a good dream about a male therapist who held me. I felt safe and warm. I knew he wouldn't hurt me or touch me inappropriately. I've been carrying the dream with me all day. Such a comforting presence, so real and familiar as if he were someone I knew in real life, but he doesn't resemble anyone I know. The feel of him in my mind is so vivid, like a good, comforting smell.

OCTOBER 26

A dream last night: Dad was leading a group of both men and women. I was sitting on the floor near his chair. There was a bottle of conditioner called "Total Control," and it made me so mad I wanted to throw it against the wall. I woke up feeling sick to my stomach.

NOVEMBER 3

When I got my period, I was glad and proud. I felt like I'd crossed a threshold and was a part of womanhood. Then Ted raped me. That good feeling of being part of a mystery turned into something horrible. Being a woman meant being raped. My body didn't belong to me. It was different from Mama's sexual abuse, which was part of a punishment. Though it felt sexual, it wasn't my kind of sexual. It bore no resemblance to my fantasies and expectations about boy-girl, man-woman sex. But Ted was a man, and the rape replaced those tentative, pleasurable images of something in the future with an opposite, horrific present reality.

I felt uncomfortable around boys because of Ted's earlier sexual abuse. But after the rape, what was uncomfortable became dangerous.

NOVEMBER 8

I dreamt that Eugene was in this apartment. I took his keys and told him that I was going out and that he'd better be gone when I came back or I'd call the police because he had no right to be there.

NOVEMBER 9

I dreamt that Gail and I were playing a board game with a couple of other people. I said to her that I wanted only to have nice thoughts in my head, to have so many nice thoughts that there was no more room for nasty thoughts. They were all gone because there was no more room for them. Gail said that was up to me. If I wanted to I could do it, but that would mean the end of therapy. Then I cried.

NOVEMBER 10

I am angry at Eugene. He was a spider, injecting me with his hooks until I was anesthetized. Then he wrapped me in threads of confusion and inadequacy and proceeded to consume me. I hate him. I never ever ever want to go through that again. I am angry that I was so abandoned in my family that I fell for his hooks. I'm angry at the lies: that my family was special and superior, that there was a desirability in this isolating difference, that I couldn't belong because I wasn't good enough for it.

Thank God I didn't belong. It was the difference of arrogance, conceit, abuse and incest. That is what I found in Eugene's web, so much like Mama's.

NOVEMBER 15

It's been such a nice day, surprising because I left my session feeling endlessly sad. I came home and played the piano, singing "Never-Never Land" over and over. My voice got higher and louder until I laughed, feeling happy. The happiness and laughter and singing and energy just kept growing all afternoon. When Janet and I were swimming, I went on singing, laughing, and crowing. Out of the pool too, while showering and changing and walking in the rain to pick up a video. So much good feeling. So much love is water.

NOVEMBER 22

In group last night I got really mad and *yelled* at Eugene, Mama and Ted. I imagined that Mama and Ted were behind Eugene, all of them pushing at me. I pushed them back and shouted them away! I felt the grown-up me through it all, giving me strength even when I felt like I was there. Afterward I was scared at first because I'd done the forbidden thing and nothing bad happened. Something in me was gone and I felt a freedom instead. Then I was no longer scared. I felt five years old and happy as though the big me pushed away all the bad people and said "all clear." The little me peeped out — "oh." So nice. I felt like that little me again when I told Gail about it today. She said I looked sparkly. During my session, I imagined Mama as a fat white spider on the floor. I walked over to that spot and squashed her with my foot. I imagined her squashed, bubbling "glub-glub." It felt good.

NOVEMBER 23

My grant period is just about half over. I start teaching again in three months. Time is going by so fast. I love what I'm doing! I was worried about structure, but writing my book is providing that. I'm so involved in creating this book, how will I end it?

XXIV

Pyrogenic

Endings involve change. What has been is no more, creating a vacuum which begs to be filled. The risk of what will fill the emptiness can be frightening. It is safer to replace loss with something that resembles it and the closer the resemblance, the safer it is. Ending is avoided, grief is stopped and change does not occur. But neither does growth.

To deal constructively with endings, we grieve our loss and leave it behind by feeling and expressing the emotions that our loss engenders. These feelings let us know how the loss affects us, raising questions about the emptiness it leaves. Though it takes time, eventually we get to the question: can the emptiness take in new life? When we can say yes, we are ready to go on and grow, finding answers that reflect our unique nature. As we adjust to the change, we recover hope. A new beginning is created, a new phase of our lives to grow in.

Those of us brought up in abusive homes did not learn this process. In recovering, we acquire the skills we need to deal with endings so that we can enjoy beginnings. We learn to grieve. We discover how to pace ourselves and take acceptable risks in making changes. We integrate and develop our many sides, gaining the flexibility we need to accommodate changes outside our control. Able to rely on ourselves and our relationships, we can face the unknown. In time we allow childhood hopes and wishes to die. We leave the endless loop, free to begin adult lives with new dreams.

When I started therapy, my inability to deal with losses gave me little tolerance for endings. I felt that all endings, however small, were catastrophic and any loss was beyond bearing. Three and a half years gave me a lot of practice in dealing with my losses. I learned to grieve, which released me to make enormous changes in myself and my life. These changes brought new experiences and with them new attitudes.

241

I believed in my ability to make something good of endings, which I could carry into the beginnings I knew would follow. Still I found endings difficult. As fall drew to a close, I felt encircled by endings: the year, my book, deciding to leave group, and, most importantly, the cancer diagnosis of Ann's mother. Her illness was painful, not only because of my love for Ann, but also because it sparked another ending: the dying hope that I could be as close to my family as she had been with her mother.

I didn't like the losses thrown at me by these endings. But I had the skills to deal with them. I talked. I wrote. I cried. I thought. I dreamt. I gradually worked my way through the tangle of feelings and questions provoked by my grief. Out of this work came physical, emotional and spiritual growth, which brought peace, understanding, courage and hope. These gave me what I needed to leave behind all that was finished and embrace the new beginnings which arose in their place.

*   *   *   *   *

NOVEMBER 24

I read some psalms last night before bed. They touched the place of peace in my centre where for so long there was only pain. I cried and cried with a sense of beauty, love and gratefulness that I am not alone. Also amazement. Like — "You mean it's going to be okay? You'll be there for me? I'm not alone in a void? Wow!!!"

I saw the B.C. ballet yesterday. They were very interesting, doing a lot with shapes. One short piece, "Urlicht (Primal Light),"[1] was worshipful, like a dance version of the great song of life. My favourite was the last piece, a funny, touching, dramatic dance about the child in all of us.

---

1 "Urlicht (Primal Light)," choreographed by William Forsythe, Ballet British Columbia.

NOVEMBER 26

A dream: I was walking with Ann and her Dad. He was wearing a white cardigan and I had my arm in his. Ann is despondent about her Mum and worried about her brother. I say something hopeful. She says her gums are swollen and her teeth will fall out. Her Dad says not necessarily. Ann says she doesn't want to hear this stuff. I say, "So just be sad." She cries hard. Her Dad is now walking behind us. I rub her back and hold her hand, saying, "Be sad. It's okay." She says, "I love my Mum and she's going to die." She cries. Something is on the road — a giant butterfly. It turns into a man wearing a bright costume, cartwheeling across the road. Ann says he could be killed. Then she says she doesn't want to hurt my feelings but don't say it's okay. and then say something opposite. I thought of how to answer. I wasn't saying opposite things and asked myself why Ann thought so. There must be something more than met the eye. I wondered what. Then I woke up. This dream disturbs me. Is it a reminder of my grief? About crying and going on? Sadness gives rise to the butterfly.

NOVEMBER 27

Ann's mum is having her operation right now. Ann told me two weeks ago that her mother has cancer. It tears me up to hear the depth of Ann's hurt. I'm sad myself. And angry. It's so unfair. Why couldn't she have twenty years off Mama's life or Eugene's? What's the point, the meaning, is there any?

Dear God, I hope Ann's mum is okay.

NOVEMBER 29

The forbidden thing is not only to speak the truth, but also to leave behind the lies and the abuse.

NOVEMBER 30

John Bradshaw, talking about family roles, described the child who is like the scapegoat in ancient Israel, smeared with blood by the high priest, sent off into the desert with the people's sins. It perfectly describes my position in the family. It is almost literal in the way I'm here and they all live in another city.

During group that image came into my mind. I could see it so clearly. The little goat, me, in the desert, clip-clop, sand all around, scared, alone, nothing to drink. Then I realized I wasn't alone. I had myself. God was with me. In my worst moments, in the wasteland, I felt at my core the presence of loving infinity, encouraging me to find what I needed to survive. It was inside of me through therapy, as my soul unfolded, steadying me, strengthening me to face whatever came. The eternal poured through me like spring water, the abundance of my blessings: comfort, love, friendship. Never again will I be separated from this wellspring of my being.

Tears poured from my eyes. Anna was wonderful, hand on my back, rubbing my shoulder, petting me while I quietly cried. I was a little afraid to talk about it in group because I know there are women whose fathers are religious and abused them. It's hard for me too that I connect religion with Ted's *frumkeit* (religiosity). But I described what I saw and felt. I was warmed by the responsiveness of the women in group.

When I talked to Gail about it, tears ran down now and again until the end, when I sobbed and sobbed, Gail patting my back. I love her. A picture came into my mind, a scene from "Bontsha the Silent." God and the angels were welcoming me, all light and music, and like a trumpet, loud and proud: "And I shall dwell in the house of the Eternal forever." I thought, Bontsha couldn't speak, but I can. I do. I asked Gail for a hug and it was good. She smiled full at me and I felt loved.

So that's it. I've reached page 2,000 in my journal and I see a symbol of welcome. What a nice way to reach page 2,000.

DECEMBER 2

I feel so good tonight. I have such a peaceful, loving feeling inside me. Is this contentment?

DECEMBER 7

For the first time since I can remember, I am not hooked into *any* users!

DECEMBER 9

Seeing Wanda and Gary with the babies in domestic bliss spurred my interest in dating. They offered to fix me up with Gary's brother. I agreed, though thinking about it, my mind wanders into memories of Eugene. What I have to remember is that I can trust myself. I'm not alone. Going out with men is scary because it's new and I had such a horrible marriage. But I'm different. I'm aware. I can feel the giving up and helping inclinations, which means I can deal with them. They will not take me over.

DECEMBER 17

Janet and I went dancing last night. I had a good time, better than last because I was more comfortable, less demanding of myself, relaxed.

DECEMBER 21

Ending therapy has always meant abandonment to me. I simply couldn't see it any other way. I was afraid to even bring the subject up for fear Gail would say, "Well, I guess you're ready then. Good-bye." I've just realized that *my* objective is independence. I will choose to leave because I want to. I will leave therapy to go on to something I want more. That's what Gail meant when she compared it to graduation, but I didn't understand the concept. I saw university as a few years of freedom, which I'd have to give up for undesirable, weighty responsibilities. That's what graduation meant to me, descendence into hell, or a deeper layer of it, rather than ascendency. And that's what happened. I went on to Eugene.

There's a revolution taking place in my mind.

DECEMBER 31

I feel weepy, tender and blessed. It's a peaceful day, misty outside, dreamlike and beautiful. The year is turning into a new decade that will bring on the millennium. What will be? The Eastern bloc is radically changing. The world picture as it's been all my life is in flux. How will it settle?

Life is wonderful. I have a dazzlingly purple coat, a ski jacket and boots. I am amazed at how good it feels to have warm, dry feet.

My book has been the focus of my life this year. I hope I find a way to finish it well, going on to a new focus.

1990

JANUARY 2

Fell asleep with a headache and woke up with one. I dreamt that Mum was on her deathbed. She acknowledged the abuse and I was glad, but I'd already forgiven her and accepted that she hadn't protected me. I held her while she was dying.

JANUARY 4

Gail asked me why I wore a knee-length skirt and sweater today. I don't need to hide any more, that's why.

Because of the revolution that's been going on in my thoughts around becoming independent, I'm rethinking my criterion for ending group. I always thought I'd continue as long as I was getting something out of it. A better question might be what else could I do with my time. Could I use it better to expand my horizons? Perhaps I need to try that out. I think I might well stop after this session.

JANUARY 6

Met Gary's brother today. It was fun to go out in mixed company, but I came home so shaky, I was almost in tears. Talking to Ann and Alma, I came back to myself, though still a bit shaky — and tired.

JANUARY 9

I was up early today and exercised! Hurray! I took two skirts in to be shortened and went to a lecture on the different movements in Judaism.

JANUARY 15

Though I'm hungry for the changes I'm making in my life, I have to take it slowly so I can deal with the feelings that come up.

I miss Gail more than I thought I would. My routine is undisturbed by her holiday. I went to the zoo last week, skating yesterday. My life is no longer focused around therapy. There is a rhythm and structure to my days around exercise, work, play, weekends, etc. But I miss Gail more as time goes on. It used to be that I had the greatest difficulty at the beginning of her holiday. I think the change came about because I feel her absence differently. It's an emptiness rather than a prop withdrawn.

JANUARY 16

I now own all of me — body, soul, mind, feelings — and I own my future. I carry my past with me and it's up to me to use that in making my life worthwhile. I see this session of group as a bridge between my past and my future because it's time to go on and make that future.

JANUARY 27

I went to Sabbath services this morning. I really enjoyed it: enough traditional to feel homey and enough new to add meaning. A couple of times I had tears in my eyes, so gently touched in the centre part of me. It was hard to go and hard to be there. Every man with a beard reminded me of Ted. I came home and slept for hours with a headache. I'm fine now, looking forward to group (how times have changed!) and seeing Gail. I want to get all this stirred up stuff off my chest to disentangle these aspects of life from the abuse and make them my own. I don't want my enjoyment of beauty and peace on the Sabbath tainted by memories of jerks.

I feel vulnerable, soft, open, wide-eyed. But I am also grown-up and able to take care of myself. I can be open and I can be closed by choosing where it's right for me.

I wore one of my shortened skirts today. I felt good. I've bought a full length mirror and I like to see myself, mostly. I enjoy this coming into the world as a woman, but right now it's difficult, bringing close the memories of sexual abuse.

JANUARY 29

I got home late, couldn't sleep, ending up at three in the morning with a full blown case of the freezing heebie-jeebies. A hot bath and all my calming techniques got me to sleep. I felt smack in the past last night, teetering on the edge most of the day. I made up my mind midafternoon to just relax and ride it through. Reading helped get my mind out of the terror into the safety of the present. Every time I close my eyes, I feel crowded by memories of being touched. I hate it. I tell myself they can't touch me now. I'm safe. I'm grown-up. I'm making bigger muscles by exercising.

JANUARY 30

Deciding to leave group was easier before this session started. I don't miss group between times. Now I'm conscious of what a safe place it is for me and how much I've got there. It makes me sad to leave group. It's scary to leave the nest.

JANUARY 31

Last night I dreamt I was pregnant. When my water broke I called Mum because I was scared. My feelings were stronger than my fears of rejection. Then the baby was there. I wasn't sure if it was okay or not. The doctor said it was "pyrogenic." After I woke up, I thought it must have a fiery spirit.

XXV

Ordinary Wonders

To my surprise, "pyrogenic" is a real word. It means producing or produced by fire. Like all of us who recover from abuse, I was reborn out of the fires of my past, transformed from the cause of torment to a source of power. This is not to say that my past would never hurt again. But the past would have a different meaning in my life. It was not the unconscious guiding force. It was not the weight that held me down. It was my past, from which I had suffered, and out of which I had drawn the courage to be reborn.

Like everyone, I have weaknesses because of who I am and where I've come from. But I also have strength and knowledge. Like all survivors, I have the strength gained through endurance and the labour of recovery. I have the knowledge of what survival and healing entail. Knowing what abuse is, knowing what lies are, knowing my true self, I sifted through the experiences of my childhood to find the good that is there: the lessons of love, the values I respect, the qualities I admire. I have known good and evil. I gained the strength to face it, to respond as I choose, to build a life of integrity and richness. This is my legacy, and the legacy of all survivors.

The views, dreams, character, I'd brought into therapy had matured. The child masquerading as a grownup was no more. In her place stood an adult with tender regard for the child part of my nature. I no longer needed my family. My childhood was over. I had found a place for myself, apart from them. Even so, it was tough to let them go their way, while I went on my own.

God be with you; fare well. These words of forgiveness were so hard for me, releasing my family from owing me my childhood, releasing myself from the driving wish to obtain it. In saying goodbye, I would leave my grandmother dead and buried. I would leave my brother to his God and my sister to her success, hoping that he did minimal damage and that she found peace. I would leave my parents their limitations, saluting them, survivors who taught me to survive, passing on to me precious gifts which enabled me to do so much more.

In my corner of the world, I was getting involved in new activities that filled my adult desires to belong, to be sexual, to be intimate, to do meaningful work. Though these activities stirred up memories that confronted me with unfinished business, memories could no longer paralyse me. I was able to deal with them and continue to expand my horizons, making my corner of the world a tremendous place to be.

* * * * *

JANUARY 31

I'm afraid that in associating with other Jews, I'll be ostracized for who I am and what I believe, the way my family ostracized me. I feel like Ted belongs in synagogue and I don't. Isn't that awful!? I feel soiled.

FEBRUARY 4

Thinking that Ted belongs and I don't is my family's bullshit. It makes me angry! They're the ones who looked at my religious observance as eccentricity, but revere his.

It is hard to realize that other Jews can accept my reality. The synagogue community is an extended family. By welcoming me, it shows up the dysfunction in my family. I have a sense of what I have lost, the nurturing in a Jewish home. Like everything else, this intrinsic part of our shared identity was used to back up the family script. Shame on them, no shame to me. In all fairness, they showed me the beauty and history in Judaism, which is why I love Passover so much. But they also used it to keep each of us in our place. It makes me mad. To twist what is holy for the service of abuse. To make what is supposed to help us be our best selves support hell. It makes me sad too. How deeply sad.

FEBRUARY 7

The family myth said Dad was on my side. In some ways he was. But he also bought my role as the crazy one. I felt loved by him and I felt special because he loved me with my craziness. We were close and Mum encouraged that. But Dad could also be cool and dismissive.

Mum and I were supposed to be opposites in conflict. There was some validity to that. But also falseness. Though the family myth said that Dad and I were a pair, Mum and I are alike in a lot of ways. We share many views around Judaism, womanhood and the importance of speaking out. We don't like to keep things inside. We share a sense of fun and spontaneity. She taught me that I could do whatever I set my mind to. I like her style.

FEBRUARY 13

What does it mean to say goodbye? Letting go and going on, certainly. But what do those words mean? Because my family wouldn't let me go, I've had to wrest myself from their grasp and it feels like a nauseating tearing.

Dear God, help me do this thing. I know it's not something that happens in a moment. I've been doing it since I started therapy, maybe since I left home. What marks the final closing of the door?

I've asked so many times in so many ways — who am I?

I'm a person with my unique nature, my feelings, thoughts and dreams. I'm a writer. That is the work of my soul. I'm a woman. That is the gender and body of my soul. I'm a Jew. That is the roots of my soul. And what do I do with these things — the work, gender, body, roots? What do I make of it?

I make something that takes my family with me and leaves them behind. You are in me, in my writing, in my expression as a woman, in my roots. You can never leave me, but you are also never with me. I do not leave you and I leave you utterly because my life is mine, containing the gifts you gave me. I reject the curse that keeps you bunched together. You can't grow like that, not well anyway.

I love you and I choose to leave you. You did not encourage my independence. You said I must be crazy or sick to leave home. But I will leave you because I love myself enough to create the sendoff you never gave me. It's hard. I want so much for you to see me leave, to wave goodbye, to be proud that I can make a life that's full and worthwhile. You gave me the wherewithal to do that and I thank you. But I have to walk on, alone. Dear God, help me do that. Help me walk into the future.

FEBRUARY 16

I think the closing of the door occurs partly by saying goodbye through expressing my feelings and thoughts about what I'm leaving. But it also occurs by doing it. In going on with my life, writing, dating, going to synagogue, and all the things that make a full satisfying life for me, I am saying goodbye and closing the door behind me.

FEBRUARY 17

It's such a good feeling to like my body. My knees have joined the world and I have given up big, loose sweaters for blouses and sweaters that are shorter, fitting closer to the body. This is *so* much fun.

FEBRUARY 21

Ann's mother is dying. I feel for Ann. I'm doing my best to be there for her. I watch the cloud hanging over, impending doom. I dread the suffering Ann will experience when Dottsie dies, the long days of mourning. I'm scared of having to face my own feelings about death, to stare down my fears and face reality. I'm sad too on my own behalf.

FEBRUARY 25

I feel terribly nauseous. Headache too. Notes because too sick to write full sentences. Saw *Half the Kingdom*[1] at downtown synagogue. Film of Jewish women talking about feelings as women, as Jews. Many are my feelings too. Good film, moving, met some nice people.

---

1 *Half The Kingdom*, directed by Francine E. Zuckerman and Roushell N. Goldstein, Kol Ishah Productions Inc. with the National Film Board of Canada, Studio D, 1989.

Young man, new born *frumer* (observant Jew), sanctimonious, self-righteous — bleah! Reminds me of Ted. Gives me headache. Makes me ill. But I put him in his place, once nicely, once snarky. Good for me! Talked to Mum about death. She shows wisdom, respect, understanding. Nice. Nice. Makes me suddenly very sick. Why? Turned upside down? My world is wrong? *No.* Mum has grown and so have I. On this subject we can discuss, others still taboo. Mum compliments me, so strange. I thank her for help re Ann's mother. Too much nice is so strange. Put down man like Ted, other people cheer — unfamiliar. Mum and I talk nice is so strange. Where is mistreatment? In the past as child, and then as adult child, unable to defend myself, frightened, couldn't communicate clearly as true self. Now can. Being me is good and good is strange. Dizzy and nauseous. But it's OKAY!

FEBRUARY 28

I am still grappling with the knowledge that Dottsie is dying, but at least I don't feel oppressed and weighed down by sadness the way I have been. I find that talking about my feelings helps (surprise, surprise, you'd think after all this time in therapy I'd be clued in to that). While I haven't had much to do with Dottsie directly, she is very present in my relationship with Ann. Often a part of our conversation, a reference point, a source of validation. When Ann told me, for instance, that Dottsie gave me a lot of credit for leaving Eugene and thought it was amazing I could, I felt much better about the years I couldn't leave, and being able to at last. Dottsie, like Ann, has a load of common sense. She's real and lives in reality. And she has gumption. I'll miss her.

In my wrestle with mortality, I call to mind the abuse. It's not something I wish was part of my life, but I can grow something good out of it. I think I can give death meaning in the same way. I admire Dottsie. Maybe one of the ways I can honour her life is to work at emulating the qualities I admire.

MARCH 7

I've made arrangements to take someone out for lunch so I can get his advice on publishing. I am well-suited to this chancy business I'm entering. I can work to make my dreams come true.

Dear God, give me the strength to take the risks I must in order to make that happen. Give me the strength to bear disappointment and failure. Give me patience and hope. Wish me good luck.

I don't know why I'm crying so much. Well, that's one good thing about computerizing my journal. I can cry and write at the same time.

MARCH 14

I am testing the lessons I learned in group: that I am acceptable, that I can belong. Allowing myself to feel the gestures of welcome from the congregation is unfamiliar. I want to belong. I believe I can but I'm afraid I might not be accepted, and the particular reminders of my family are painful.

I was thinking last night about the war and Mum and Dad. Growing up, the Holocaust enveloped me. I felt like my life was a dot inside it. Now my life is large and it's the dot. The Holocaust is important because it formed some of my values about prejudice and taking a stand. It's important because, along with their childhoods, it formed Mum and Dad, disabling them so they couldn't give me what I needed as a child. From one angle, Mum and Dad did terrifically well, given where they came from and what they went through. They gave me some solid values, some real strengths and gifts. Looked at from another angle, they allowed me to be abused. That's the way it is.

MARCH 17

I'm beginning to know more people at the synagogue and it feels good.

MARCH 18

Thinking about ending therapy, I realized it's no more a magical event than anything else I've experienced in the healing process. It is part of my evolution. Everything that makes up life leaves a mark, changes our path. We can't anticipate how or what we make of it till we do. I'm not great at accepting the unknown, but if I knew everything what would be the point of life?

MARCH 19

I'm sad. Dottsie died this morning at 5:30. So now it begins. Grief is hard. Dear God, help me be a good friend to Ann. I know I can't take away her sorrow or help her grieve. That's hers alone. But let me be the kind of shoulder she can lean on. Let me be some good to her, please. Help me find the words and actions to give what she needs from me in this time.

MARCH 20

Last night I dreamt that Mum was holding me from behind. It felt good. I said I was glad that Mama was dead, but I was sad that Mum was. Then I realized that it was Ann's mother who died, not mine. With her died the hope that my mother could be like her.

In group Anna suggested I speak as the little kid in me and answer as the grownup. Giving voice to the kid, I said I didn't want anyone but Mum and Dad. As the grownup, I answered that I simply couldn't have them. The abuse happened a long time ago. It's over. It can't be rectified and I can never have the childhood I wanted. But I can have other people now to nurture me and share my life. So I said goodbye from the little kid in me, picturing Mum and Dad as ghosts looking like they did in my childhood, then as images of dust the wind blew away. Instead of the images, I then saw Mum and Dad as they are now. I cried in Anna's arms. It felt good to lean on her, held by her, while I cried. I've cried so many times in her arms. All those times have added together in warmth, trust and love.

By giving up the fantasy of Mum and Dad as I wished them to be, I gain the reality. I love Mum and Dad for who they are.

I have an image in my mind. Mum stands behind me, her hand on my shoulder. We are dancing, and behind her stretch ribbons of women dancing with us: all the women before us, Dad's mother, his sisters, Mama, good and bad dancers, they are all a part of the dance. This dance is *Simkha*,[2] celebration.

MARCH 22

My book is the moving finger that writes and moves on. I must have faith that it will do what needs to be done, saying what needs to be said, revealing the truth I have to see and know. It will have the meaning in my life that I need from it.

MARCH 29

Group is over. And my book is ending. I'm scared, sad, and exhilarated by turns. Tuesday I got more than I hoped for, i.e. the good wishes, people in the group waving goodbye: the sendoff I didn't get at home. I got that and more.

After I read what I'd prepared, the first page of my journal, an excerpt from "Caring," and the poem I wrote to end group, I talked about all the people who weren't there, saying goodbye to them. I had a picture in my mind of those I've met in group who've come and gone. They've all given me much too. Then I said goodbye to each person in group by telling her what I felt deepest in my heart, my feelings, wishes for her, what she'd given me, her importance for me in group.

I hadn't anticipated their reaction. Each person in turn talked about what I'd given her, what she'd learned from me, appreciated about me. I feel warmed by that, and tender.

We had a closing exercise, writing what we'd say as a wise woman talking to a seven-year old child. We each took a flower from the gorgeous vase Anna brought, and read our piece. I picked a great pink daisy, pink for hope and beginnings. It was hard to take the flower. I didn't want to do it, then thought of giving it away, as if by doing that I wouldn't be leaving. But then I'd also have to give up the beginning that the flower represents. Here is what I wrote:

---

2 *Simkha* is a Hebrew word that means happiness and festive occasion, like a birth or wedding.

I am the old woman of your dreams. Come into my arm's embrace. Time passes and the future waits. The scream is screamed when you walk through me into now. On the other side, you are free. We are a circle, the three of us. You can never be alone. What ends begins anew.

So this is it. My book ends. And I go on.

MARCH 29

BEGINNING

I say goodbye
to where I began
a lonely shadow hiding from ghosts
looking for miracles
amongst hard chairs and banging pipes.

Unplug the noisy clock,
it is Tuesday at seven — time stops
in this room for children
daycare is nightcare, now.
Who ran with me in the secret woods
where shadows thicken into monsters?
You
you saw the slashing claws
you heard my scream
and you stayed.

I say goodbye
to you beside me with ready arms
when monsters and trees turned
out to be those I loved.

I am comforted
who never knew what comfort was
trembling with discovery
miracles of holding, tears, aching eased
visible and heard — a miracle
desire — a miracle — desired — a miracle
pride
whose place was always shame
miracle of miracles.
I am the lost child found
creating worlds
I am the cowering woman upright
in command.

And now, I say goodbye to miracles.
The magic night is done.
Plug in the clock.
Time moves again.

I walk into the future morning,
belonging
to the ordinary wonders of the day.

RECOMMENDED READING

FIRST BOOKS
Outgrowing the Pain: A Book For And About Adults Abused As Children
Eliana Gil
Dell Publishing, New York, 1983.
    Simple language and humorous illustrations explain the effects of physical and sexual abuse and the recovery process.

Why Me? Help For Victims Of Child Sexual Abuse (Even If They Are Adults Now)
Lynn B. Daugherty
Mother Courage Press, Racine, 1984.
    In question and answer format, clearly and simply explains sexual abuse and healing for victims, family, friends and counsellors.

ACCOUNTS OF SEXUAL ABUSE
I Never Told Anyone: Writings by Women Survivors of Child Sexual Abuse
Edited by Ellen Bass and Louise Thornton
Harper & Row, New York, 1983.
    Anthology of stories and poems about abuse by father, foster parent, brother, grandfather, grandmother, uncle, friends and acquaintances, strangers. Each author is introduced with a brief description of her history and healing.

Kiss Daddy Good-night: Ten Years Later
Louise Armstrong
Simon & Schuster, Inc., New York, 1978, 1987.
    Speaking out on father-daughter incest.

Voices in the Night: Women Speaking About Incest
Edited by Toni A.H. McNaron and Yarrow Morgan
Cleis Press, San Francisco, 1982.

Anthology of stories and poems about experiences of incest with brother, mother, father, uncle, step-father, brother-in-law.

ACCOUNTS OF RECOVERY

Cry Hard and Swim
Jacqueline Spring
Virago Press Limited, London, 1987.

A woman's story of recovery from father-daughter incest. Inspirational.

The Ones Who Got Away: Women Who Left Abusive Partners
Ginny NiCarthy
The Seal Press, Seattle, 1987.

The stories of thirty-three women who left abusive partners to make a better life.

When You're Ready
Kathy Evert
Launch Press, Walnut Creek, 1987.

An unusual account of a woman's healing from physical and sexual abuse by her mother.

THE HEALING PROCESS

Becoming Your Own Parent: The Solution for Adult Children of Alcoholic and Other Dysfunctional Families
Dennis Wholey
Doubleday, New York, 1988.

Essays by experts plus comments from a diverse group of recovering adults.

The Courage to Heal: A Guide for Women Survivors of Child Sexual Abuse
Ellen Bass and Laura Davis

Harper & Row, New York, 1988.

An encyclopedia of healing, includes writing exercises and stories of healing from survivors of diverse backgrounds and orientations.

Healing Your Sexual Self
Janet G. Woititz
Health Communications Inc., Deerfield Beach, 1989.

Concisely addresses feelings, defenses, triggers, sexual orientation, addiction, AIDS, religion.

Incest and Sexuality: A Guide to Understanding and Healing
Wendy Maltz and Beverly Holman
Lexington Books, Lexington, 1987.

Concise and clear explanation of effects and healing: a bill of sexual rights, survivors helping themselves, partners working together, getting professional help.

Making Therapy Work: Your Guide to Choosing, Using, and Ending Therapy
Fredda Bruckner-Gordon, Barbara Kuerer Gangi, and Geraldine Urbach Wallman
Harper & Row, New York, 1988.

An excellent guide to understanding and making the most of therapy.

UNDERSTANDING INCEST AND SEXUAL ABUSE

The Best Kept Secret: Sexual Abuse of Children
Florence Rush
McGraw-Hill Book Company, New York, 1980.

The historical and sociological context of sexual abuse; a classic.

Child Sexual Abuse: New Theory and Research
David Finkelhor
Free Press, New York, 1984.

A social and psychological review of sexual abuse. Examines theories and results of researchers' studies.

Conspiracy of Silence: The Trauma of Incest
Sandra Butler
Volcano Press, Inc., San Francisco, 1978, 1985.

The dynamics of incest: victim, perpetrator, other family members and the helping professions. A respectful and informative book.

The Incest Perpetrator: A Family Member No One Wants to Treat
Edited by Anne L. Horton et al
Sage Publications, Newbury Park, 1990.

Profiles of offenders include chapters on sibling incest and female perpetrators as well as father-daughter incest. Covers treatment for offenders.

The Secret Trauma: Incest in the Lives of Girls and Women
Diana E.H. Russell
Basic Books, New York, 1986.

A study of the incidence and effects of incest on 930 women. Covers abuse by a wide range of male relatives and by women. Dispels the myth of mutuality in sibling incest, however conclusions minimize prevalence and effects of abuse by women.

Sexual Abuse of Children in the 80's
Edited by Benjamin Schlesinger
University of Toronto Press, Toronto, 1986.

Ten essays and an annotated bibliography, includes a summary of "The Badgley Report on Sexual Offenses Against Children in Canada," (1984).

VIOLENCE AGAINST WOMEN

Battered but Not Beaten: Preventing Wife Battering in Canada
Linda MacLeod
Ottawa: Canadian Advisory Council on the Status of Women, 1987.

Examines wife battering through the experiences of battered women and front line workers. Provides up to date, concrete information. Clear and sensitive. Includes bibliography.

The Battered Woman
Lenore E. Walker
Harper & Row, New York, 1979.
The how and why of battering and recovery, a good solid book packed with information.

Getting Free: A Handbook For Women In Abusive Relationships
Ginny Nicarthy
Seal Books, Seattle, 1982.
A practical self-help book that includes dealing with the abuser, children, fears, finding help, evaluating professionals and making a new life.

RELATIONSHIPS

Beyond Codependency: and getting better all the time
Melody Beattie
Harper & Row, San Francisco, 1989.
Recovery, relapse, change, relationships — a positive, down to earth book.

Too Good for her Own Good: Searching For Self And Intimacy In Important Relationships
Claudia Bepko and Jo-Ann Krestan
HarperPerennial, New York, 1991.
Socialized to be impossibly and harmfully "good," women can instead have healthy relationships without losing ourselves. Refreshing.

Women Who Love Too Much: When You Keep Wishing and Hoping He'll Change
Robin Norwood
J.P. Tarcher, Los Angeles, 1985.
Recognizing, understanding and changing the pattern of involvement in destructive relationships.

OTHER RECOMMENDED READING

*Life is Goodbye Life is Hello: Grieving Well Through All Kinds of
Loss*
Alla Bozarth-Campbell, Ph.D.
CompCare Publishers, Minneapolis, 1986.

Death, birth, parenting, change, separation, sickness, success, all
create loss: how it feels, what it does and what you can do about it.

*Necessary Losses: The Loves, Illusions, Dependencies and
Impossible Expectations That All of Us Have to Give Up in Order
to Grow*
Judith Viorst
Fawcett Gold Medal, Ballantine Books, New York, 1986.

From infancy to old age, the function and achievements of each
stage of development.

The Right to Feel Bad: Coming to Terms with Normal Depression
Lesley Hazleton
Dial Press, Garden City, 1984.

Normal depression as a necessary process in healing and maturing,
includes discussion of suicidal thoughts, the role of psychotherapy,
human vitality. An insightful, compassionate book.

Women and Self-Esteem
Linda Tschirhart Sanford and Mary Ellen Donovan
Penguin Books, New York 1985.

Explains the reasons and effects of low self-esteem in women as
a result of home life, work and social institutions. "Blue prints for
change" at the end of each chapter.